ARMY
Fitness Manual

Attention Authors

Manas Publications is fighting a war to tell the world that India can win the battle not only by the bullet but also by pen. We are converting fighters into writers. There is no dearth of intellectuals in our country. However, their knowledge is confined to them only. No sincere effort has been made by any other publisher to channelise their knowledge. That is why the talent of every intellectual remains latent. An author always presents the raw material in the shape of a manuscript and it is the job of the publisher to convert it into a completely finished book. Manas has been motivating intellectuals continually and publishing their manuscripts for more than three decades and would like to publish your manuscript too. If you or your colleagues have a manuscript ready for publication or are working on it, contact us with a detailed synopsis and list of contents. Manas can also suggest you a suitable title for writing related to your area of expertise. Manas is known for its publishing quality. We take utmost care in production and give wide publicity to the book and its author through our national and international distribution network.

ARMY
Fitness Manual

Canadian Forces
Personnel Support Agency

Manas Publications
(We Convert Fighters into Writers)
New Delhi-110002 (INDIA)

MANAS PUBLICATIONS
(We Convert Fighters into Writers)
(Publishers, Distributors, Importers & Exporters)
4402/5-A, Ansari Road (Opp. HDFC Bank)
Darya Ganj, New Delhi-110 002 (INDIA)
Off. ✆ 23260783, 23265523, Res. 23842660
Fax: 011-23272766
E-mail: manaspublications@gmail.com
manaspublications@yahoo.com

ISBN 978-81-7049-342-6
₹ 495/-

Designed at
Manas Publications

Printed in India at
HS Offsets, Delhi
and published by Mrs Suman Lata for
Manas Publications, 4402/5-A, Ansari Road,
(Opp. HDFC Bank), Darya Ganj,
New Delhi-110 002 (INDIA)

Contents

Preface 7

1. Fit to Fight 9
2. Army Fitness Training Principles 27
3. Training Prescriptions 37
4. Fine Tuning Your Programme 53
5. Training Circuits and Routines 61
6. Speciality Training Programmes 111

Index 137

Preface

The Physical fitness is fundamental to being an effective soldier in Land Force Command. It ensures vigour, alertness and stamina in operations and in the performance of your duties. Fit individuals make strong team members, ensuring operational readiness of our Army at all times. Regardless of your occupation, you can be called upon to perform difficult and dangerous tasks, whether they are combat, peace enforcement, peacekeeping, or aid to civil power. You must be ready to go on short notice and for sustained operations. The Army leadership is committed to your personal preparation for this. We will provide the guidance, equipment, time and technical support to help you train and reach the Army Fitness Standard (AFS). As a member of a field unit you are required to meet or exceed the AFS once a year and maintain this fitness level year round. Your responsibility is to effectively use the time and make the necessary effort to achieve the AFS as a minimum fitness level, and you are encouraged to go beyond it. This Army Fitness Manual provides the information you need to get the job done. Use it!

1

Fit to Fight

Soldiers need a **high** level of fitness. This includes a high aerobic capacity, muscular strength, endurance and power, flexibility, and a healthy body weight. Achieving these goals brings many benefits.

FITNESS IS..

Aerobic capacity – the ability of your lungs, heart, blood vessels, and muscles to take in oxygen, deliver it to the working muscle sand other tissues, and have the working muscles use the oxygen to provide energy for work.

Muscular strength and endurance – the ability of your muscles to generate for cesina particular movement.

Power – the ability of your muscles to generate forces at a high speed.

Contd ...

Flexibility – the ability of your muscles and joints to move through their full range.

... and a **healthy body weight.**

Leaders responsible for organizing group fitness sessions where individuals will be working in **Army Fitness Programme** activities will find some helpful information at the end of this chapter.

AEROBIC FITNESS will help you:

- work for extended periods without undue fatigue
- make sound decisions even after periods of demanding work
- recover quickly from hard work
- handle heat stress and altitude more effectively
- adjust more easily to travel and jet lag
- resist minor infections and colds
- recover more quickly from any injuries you might have.

STRENGTH AND POWER will help you:

- start, stop, and react quickly in field situations
- lift or move objects or your own body weight more often and more quickly with less fatigue
- perform twisting movements in full fighting gear
- carry objects (or casualties) over distance at speed
- protect your lower back and reduce your risk of injury.

Good FLEXIBILITY will help you:

- complete demanding tasks with less muscle soreness or discomfort
- reduce your overall risk of injury.

Maintaining a HEALTHY WEIGHT (without excess body fat) will:

- enhance your ability to do aerobic work and recover quickly from it
- allow you to move your own body weight and carry heavy objects more easily—and to move more quickly
- reduce health risks such as heart disease and diabetes and lower-back problems and other injuries.

MEETING THE ARMY FITNESS STANDARD

Fully developing all the components of fitness will have a direct impact on your performance on the AFS. Aerobic fitness, strength, power, flexibility and a healthy body weight—all together—are highly related to your ability to perform the tasks making up the AFS assessment.

The AFS is designed to ensure that you are capable of enduring the rigours of operations and, if necessary, combat. It is comprised of the following tasks.

Weightload March. March a distance of 13 km in full fighting gear and rucsack (24.5 kg total kit: ie., weapon, Equipment Issue Scale (EIS), helmet, webbing and Field pack). Complete the distance in under 2hr 26min 20s. This is equivalent to a pace of 5.33 km/hr. Your perceived exertion will be recorded throughout the march to help monitor your pace and ensure safety.

Casualty Evacuation. Lift and carry (fireman's carry) another soldier of similar weight and height a distance of 100 m, with both members wearing a helmet and carrying ammunition and a weapon. Lift with your legs and avoid excessive forward bending so you don't put undue stress on your lower back. Complete the task in less than 60 seconds.

Ammunition Box Lift. Lift 48 ammunition boxes (20.9 kg, 4B/IT) from the floor to a height of 1.3 m. You should work at a strong moderate pace and be careful to lift correctly to protect your back. Helmet only is worn for this task. Complete the task in less than five minutes.

Trench (Maximal) Dig. Using a standard shovel, move .486 cubic metres of pea gravel (1 cm in diametre) from one trench box to another. Helmet only is worn for this task. Complete the task in less than six minutes using whatever technique is comfortable and works for you.

You will be given full instructions for each task and adequate time to warm up and cool-down during the testing session. The AFS assessment is done in one session with a minimum ten-minute break between each of the four tests standards.

The **12-Week Army Fitness Programme** has been developed specifically to prepare you to reach the AFS. In order to do this ...

- It is a balanced and progressive programme that develops *all* fitness components.
- It includes both aerobic intervals and continuous aerobic training.
- It incorporates upper-body and lower-body strengthening exercises and exercises for the abdominal core.
- It involves a variety of innovative exercises to improve speed and power.
- It adds a weightload march in the later weeks of the programme to prepare you for this particular AFS task.
- It provides a series of field exercises to help with specific preparation for the other three AFS tasks.

Presently, the Land Force Command Physical Fitness Standard only includes the Weightload March and the Casualty Evacuation. The additional two tasks will be added in the future and changes in equipment or resources may require adjustments to the standards.

BUILDING ON THE BASICS

This programme builds on the CF EXPRES Programme and takes you to a higher level of fitness. The CFMPFS uses a predictive test model—including the 20-metre shuttle run, hand-grip, push-up and sit-up— to determine the fitness levels required, by age and gender, to meet the five tasks common to all soldiers. Since the normal physical abilities of young, middle-age, and older individuals can vary—and that of men and women varies, too—the fitness standards in the CFMPFS also vary.

The AFS is different. It uses the task performance model to determine the fitness level of each soldier. *Every* soldier—young or old, male or female, small or large—must be able to meet the standards to be fit to fight. This means that to meet the AFS, *all* soldiers have to develop their endurance, strength, power, and flexibility to the appropriate level as shown in the Fitness Check table in Chapter 4. If there were lower fitness requirements for older soldiers, smaller people, or women, then these individuals would be performing the AFS tasks at closer to their maximum capacity. This means they would fatigue sooner, they would be at greater personal risk, and they could jeopardize the welfare of others in their unit in a real-life situation.

THE AFS DIFFERENCE ...

Every soldier—young or old, male or female, small or large—must be able to meet the AFS to be fit to fight.

Special Guidance for Female Soldiers

Land Force Command recognizes that some female soldiers may have special concerns about training and preparation for the AFS. It is well known that, generally, women do not have the same aerobic capacity as men, nor are they as strong, especially in the upper body. These differences in physical performance are due in large part to differences in body size and composition.

However, women's bodies respond to aerobic and strength training programmes in similar ways to men's. Thus, the **Army Fitness Programme** is designed to accommodate and prepare *all* soldiers for the AFS. To help with this, three load options are provided in the Bench Press and Squat items in the Fitness Check and a special upper-body strength and aerobics circuit is provided for Day 6 (Optional). Here is a little more information and advice:

Aerobic capacity: The lower aerobic capacity of women (compared to men) is due to a smaller muscle mass, a smaller volume of blood, and lower hemoglobin concentrations in the blood. In spite of this, the AFS is as attainable for women as it is for men. The **Special Upper-Body Strength and Aerobics Circuit** will help you improve both of these fitness components at the same time.

Strength improvement: Female soldiers may be concerned that they are not as strong as their male colleagues, yet they must be able to lift the same loads. Women are generally about two-thirds as strong as men, but relative to their size women can gain as much or more strength than men following similar training programmes. The good news is... the **Army Fitness Programme** will lead to significant improvement in muscular strength and endurance and help you achieve the level you need to perform to the AFS. You can use the appropriate loads in the **Fitness Check** Bench Press and Squat items and, of course, the training routines are individualized and progressive for best results.

Pregnancy: Pregnancy causes many bodily changes. Pregnant soldiers will be taken out of the regular fitness programme and will have their programmes developed and directed by PSP staff under the supervision of their base or unit medical officer.

Prescription for Success

If you follow the programme as outlined, it will help you to meet the AFS *and* prepare you for the heavy demands of field exercises and overseas deployment.

You will determine your level of readiness for the programme in Week 1 and check your progress during Weeks 5 and 9 using simple fitness checks and a four-level scoring system. The programme is designed in such a way that if you achieve Level 2 you can be reasonably assured that you have the fitness and skills necessary to meet the individual demands of each AFS task (level 1 is roughly equivalent to CFMPFS).

The AFS assessment is done in one session, however, you need to target **Level 3** to give you the fitness reserve to do all four tasks.

TAILORED FOR YOU...

The programme :

- includes guidelines to keep your sessions safe, effective, and enjoyable
- checks your progress along the way so you can fine tune you refforts and get the most out of them

- integrates the specific AFS tasks to help you improve your technique and efficiency when doing them
- allows you to start at a level that's right for you *now* and build up gradually from there.

FUEL FOR FITNESS

Good foods for meals prior to exercise include vegetables and fruits, breads, pasta, potatoes, rice, soups, skinless chicken, and fish. After exercise, refuel with pasta, breads, fruit and vegetables, non-creamy sauces and soups, potatoes, rice, salads, even waffles and pancakes. Refuel with fluids too.

Maintaining a *healthy body weight* will make it easier for you to stick to this training programme. It will also boost your energy and contribute to your general well-being. To help maintain a healthy weight:

- eat a nutritious breakfast—choose from cereals, fruit, juice, toast, and low-fat muffins
- avoid plain sugars in the form of candies, jams, soft drinks, and rich desserts
- cut down on items high in fat, such as butter, margarine, and oils, fried foods, preserved meats, and "junk food" snacks like chips and dip
- if you drink alcohol, do so in moderation.

If you feel a structured programme and group support could help in your efforts to achieve a healthy weight, ask about the **CF Weight Wellness Programme** when you pick up your copy of the *Food Guide*.

THE RIGHT STUFF ...

To fuel your training be sure to :

- eat lots of carbohydrates — pasta, grains, potatoes, fruits, and vegetables.
- get sufficient protein — it is important particularly given the programme's strength-training component.
- watch your in take of fat — oils, butter, creamy sauces, meat and the like.
- drink plenty of fluids throughout the day, especially before, during, and immediately after exercise. Water is great, and the price is right !

INJURY PREVENTION AND SAFETY

If you train sensibly, you will avoid injury and be able to stick with your programme and make good progress. Here are some tips to keep you on the right track:

Warm-up : Ease into each training session with a gentle warm-up like the one included in Chapter 5. This will prepare your body for the demands of the workout and can reduce your risk of injury during activity.

Cool-down: Finish each session with stretching exercises. This helps your body "slow down" after the workout and can reduce unnecessary stiffness and soreness that may result from vigorous activity.

Dress right: Wear comfortable clothing that doesn't restrict your movement. Dress appropriately for your activity *and* the weather (if you are outside).

Treat your feet: For running and for the strength, speed, and power routines, wear runners that have a thick sole for cushioning and good heel and arch support. Wear clean, thick cotton socks (with no holes in them!). Do not run in boots! For marches, wear boots that offer a good fit and are broken in.

Don't overdo it: The rest days are an important part of the programme so you don't over train, get too tired, and risk injury. Look for progress over a period of time, *not* for instant results.

LOOK AFTER YOUR BACK ...

Protect your back from undue stress during lifting, carrying, and all your other dynamic activities. Assume a posture that respects the back's natural, gentle curve. Avoid extreme positions.

Face objects and use your legs when you lift. Turn by moving your feet. Don't plant them and twist.

During aerobic activity...

- Do your running on grass fields, running tracks, sidewalks or flat roads. Avoid uneven and rugged surfaces.
- Run in a way that is natural and right for you—assume an erect but relaxed posture and use a comfortable stride length.
- When it's hot, drink plenty of fluids before and during activity. Look for shady running routes and watch your level of activity on extremely hot days.
- When it's cold, protect yourself from the wind as much as possible and be careful on icy surfaces. Wear several layers of clothing, gloves, and a wool toque to cover your head and ears.

During strength training...

- Learn the proper technique in each of the exercises. Use light loads when you are learning new exercises and be careful moving the weight to the starting position when using free weights.
- With free weights, be sure the collars are tight so the weights are secure on the bar. Make sure the support pin is fully inserted when using stack weights.
- Breathe comfortably—don't hold your breath. Inhale and exhale on every repetition, inhaling on the preparation phase and exhaling on the effort phase.
- Work with a partner so that you can spot each other, especially when using free weights. Adjust racks, benches, etc., so you are always in a comfortable, secure position.

During power and speed workouts...

- Ease into the plyometrics and speed routines if you don't normally do this sort of thing. Be sure to do a good cool-down stretch after the session to reduce any soreness that may result.

Warm-up/cool-down exercises are an essential part of your overall training programme. They are important for preparation, injury prevention, and comfort around each training session. They will also help you improve and maintain an adequate level of flexibility. Give these exercises the attention they deserve.

INJURY MANAGEMENT

If you do sustain an injury, act quickly to minimize damage and speed up recovery (see **RICE It** for the steps to take). If necessary, visit the Medical Inspection Room for assessment and follow the advice provided. Don't let things get worse through lack of proper care.

RICE IT...

For immediate treatment of joint and muscle injuries:

Rest the injured body part.

Ice the injured body part (10 - 20 min. every few hours).

Compress the injured area with an elastic bandage or to wel if swelling occurs.

Elevate the injured area above heart level .

Sticking with Your Programme

This training programme has been designed to prepare you for the AFS. But the sole purpose isn't just to reach the required standard. Fitness training should be enjoyable in its own right, so great effort has been taken to make sure the programme is interesting and challenging.

Nevertheless, it's natural to have low points in your training from time to time. If you have been ill, very busy, or tired, you may find you are not progressing as quickly as you would like. The winter "doldrums" can take its toll too. Any of these situations can dull your enthusiasm for training temporarily.

There are all sorts of things you can do to keep your programme on track. Here are a few suggestions:

- Train with a partner or in a group whenever you can. This will make it a fun, social time, and friendly challenges can spur you on to a greater effort.
- Change your run or march routes/location when you need some variety. But don't be tempted to switch to another activity like swimming or cycling. The running in this programme is specific to the weightload march demands of the AFS, and changing aerobic activities could jeopardize your preparation. You are, of course, welcome to do other activities you enjoy on your active rest and sports days.
- Use the **Personal Training Record** to track your workouts. This will ensure you increase training loads regularly, help you progress at the fastest possible pace, *and* keep you motivated!
- Don't rush. Set aside enough time for your activity. Appointments or other commitments pressing your session can make you a clock watcher and spoil your training time.
- If necessary, modify your programme if you have been ill and unable to train for a while. You can repeat the Week you completed most recently *or* adjust the current Week's routine by using lighter loads in the strength training circuits and a slower pace in the aerobic interval or continuous aerobic workouts, for example.

- Look for improvement over the full programme, not overnight. Depending on your initial fitness level, you may have to go through the 12-week routine more than once to get ready to meet the AFS. Fitness is an individual thing, so be patient.

GETTING EXTRA HELP...

If you are doing the programme without supervision, you may have questions or concerns along the way. If so, a member of your local CFPSA Fitness Staff can offer you guidance and advice .

Final Reminders

To pursue the programme...

- Review the **Training Principles** in the next chapter so you understand the programme structure and the methods used for aerobic, strength, and power/speed training.
- Consult the appropriate **Training Prescription** chart in Chapter 3 *every* session for programme directions. Read the introductory information to see how they are organized.
- Use the **Fine Tuning Your Programme** information from Chapter 4 in Weeks 1, 5, and 9 to monitor your progress and improvement.
- Rely on the **Warm-up and Stretching** section from Chapter 5 *every* training session for good warm-up and cool-down activities.

STAYING ON TRACK...

Follow the training principles outlined here when you workout and you will make good progress.

Tips for Fitness Leaders

The **Army Fitness Programme** is an individualized routine to help prepare each person to reach the AFS. Yet Army fitness training, by its nature, is chiefly done in a group setting. Group and unit leaders have a real responsibility, then, to ensure that each individual gets the most out of his/her training time. Whether organizing activities for a few people or for a group of 25, there are things leaders can do to ensure the programme runs smoothly. Here are a few suggestions:

- **Lead by example.** Pursue your own programme with enthusiasm. Study this manual carefully so you are knowledgeable in all its aspects and can answer questions with confidence.
- **Be prepared.** Plan ahead for each session. Assess the equipment available and decide how the session needs to be organized so your charges can work efficiently to complete their programmes within an hour. The alternative exercises in Chapter 5 can be helpful when there is a large group *and* limited formal weight-training equipment available.
- **Create a comfortable atmosphere.** Recognize that everyone is different and will progress at their own pace. Help participants choose and use the equipment that will be most comfortable and appropriate for them. Show a real interest in their individual progress. Answer questions carefully and provide encouraging, positive feedback.

- **Encourage team work.** Get them working in pairs or small groups to support one another. This creates good spirit and instills a sense of teamwork, which is so important in field and combat situations.
- **Manage the group effectively.** Doing the **Army Fitness Programme** in a group setting is different than conducting a class where everyone follows the leader or does the same thing. Your management tasks will be to keep everyone moving toward their individual goals. Using a circuit-training approach for the strength and power activities, for example, is a way to make sure everyone is active and there is no delay in waiting for specific pieces of equipment.
- **Promote a safe and effective programme.** Make sure participants do a proper warm-up at the beginning of each session and a cool-down at the end. As it is designed, the programme ensures a gradual build-up in intensity. Make sure they don't push too hard or rush. Watch them as they pursue the various strength and power activities, and offer suggestions on proper technique if necessary. All of this will help minimize the risk of injuries.
- **Maintain motivation.** Make some changes in the routine if participants are losing their enthusiasm. Do the aerobic sessions in a different setting. Use the alternative exercises instead of stack weights or free weights for a while. Devise some friendly challenges and competitions. Review the **Fitness Checks** with individuals to remind them of the progress they are making. Ask them how they are feeling. A good fitness programme brings a wonderful sense of health and well-being.

- **Be qualified.** Fitness leaders must be qualified either Primary Leadership Qualification (PLQ) Module 1, Basic Fitness Training Assistant (BFTA), Advanced Fitness Training Assistant (AFTA), Common Army Phase (CAP), or Army Operations Course (AOC) to conduct physical training / physical fitness training.

REMEMBER...

Fitness leaders should remember the 3 "F"s— **Fair, Firm, Friendly**.

2

Army Fitness Training Principles

Understanding the structure of this programme and following a few key principles when you train will reward you with good progress. Here's what you need to know to pursue the programme with success.

Aerobics :

The programme uses **continuous activity**, **interval training** and **weightload marches** to develop your aerobic fitness.

THE SET-UP...

- Day 1 of each week is generally devoted to **interval training.** This involves periods of higher-intensity *work* followed by an *easy* recovery interval (for the easy recovery interval, you can jog slowly, walk, even stop and stretch if you wish). The length of the work interval and the number of repetitions of them increase gradually over the training cycle.

- Day 5 of each week is devoted to **continuous aerobic activity** in the form of distance runs. This involves moderate-intensity work sustained over a period of time. The length of the session increases gradually over the training cycle. You will go at a pace where you are just able to talk without laboured breathing—"just talk" or "JT" as it is called.
- **Weightload marches** enter the programme on Day 5 of Weeks 7 and 8, when they take the place of your distance run. In Weeks 10, 11, and 12, the weightload march is your aerobic activity on Day 1 and Day 5. The demands of the march are increased *gradually* over the six-week period by adding weight to the load, speeding up the pace, and increasing the distance to get you ready for the AFS assessment.

DOING IT...

- **Aerobic intervals:** The approximate distance you should cover during each work interval is based on the level you achieve in the 2400 m run as shown on the **Fitness Check** chart. These distances are noted in the **Guidelines** for the **Training Prescription** charts for Weeks 1-4 and 5-8.
- **Continuous aerobic:** Your approximate pace (in metres per minute) is determined by the level you achieve in the 5 km run as shown in the **Fitness Check** chart. The paces are noted in the **Guidelines** for the **Training Prescription** charts. At the beginning, if your fitness is in the Getting Started/Level 1 range, you might be alternating running and walking. As you progress you

will be running throughout the entire session at an increasing speed that still allows a "JT" pace because of your higher fitness level.

- **Weightload march:** Your march distance and rucsack weight are noted in the **Training Prescription** charts. March at the paces shown— increasing gradually from 5.0 km/hr to 6.0 km/hr over six weeks to get you ready for the 13 km march at the 5.33 km/hr pace required in the AFS.

REMEMBER...

> During your continuous aerobic activity, you will go at a pace where you are just able to talk without laboured breathing— "just talk" or "JT" as it is called.

Strength

The programme includes circuits of upper body, lower body, and abdominal core exercises to develop your basic strength.

THE SET-UP...

- Days 2 and 4 of each week focus on strength training. You will do one upper-body (UB) and one lower-body (LB) circuit most days, choosing from the routines provided. There are five UB circuit routines and five LB ones as follows: stack weights, free weights (barbells), free weights (dumbbells), body-weight exercises, and partner-resistance exercises. For strength training, use the circuits with stack or free weights as often as possible. This will allow you to control the load effectively and steadily progress. The body-weight and partner-resistance circuits are very effective too.

You can use them if equipment isn't available and for variety to keep your routine interesting and enjoyable.

- In Weeks 8, 10, 11, and 12, Day 2 is devoted to field exercises that simulate the demands of the AFS and the real-life common tasks of every soldier. This workout replaces the upper- and lower-body strength circuits normally done on this day. These exercises are described further in the **Power and Speed** section.
- Strengthening exercises for the abdominal core (AbCore) are also done regularly, following your aerobics work on Day 1 and Day 5 for the first eight weeks of the programme and on Day 6 (Optional) in Weeks 10 to 12.
- There may be times when you don't have access to the specific equipment shown in the exercise circuits. This could happen if there are large numbers of soldiers training together in a garrison setting or when you are out in the field. To help you improvise, a range of **alternative exercises** are included after the circuits in Chapter 5. You can choose from the exercises there to replace ones where the regular equipment is unavailable or if you are looking for some variety beyond the body-weight and partner exercises.

DOING IT...

- **Upper-body and lower-body circuit routines:** Do the number of sets and reps noted in the **Training Prescription** chart for *each* exercise. Work through the exercises in order, doing the first set of each one, followed by the second set, and so on. You can start the circuit with any exercise, just be sure to go through it in sequence. Also, if you are doing a circuit using weights and find that the equipment you need isn't available (or you're uncomfortable using it), you can substitute the same numbered exercise in any of the other circuits as it will work the same muscle groups.

- **Daily training structure:** Generally, you will do one UB circuit and one LB circuit each strength-training session. There are three ways you can structure it:
    1. Do the entire UB circuit (all sets), followed by the LB circuit.
    2. Do one set of the UB circuit followed by one set of LB, then repeat.
    3. Combine the two. Do Exercise #1 of UB circuit, Exercise #1 of LB, #2 of UB, #2 of LB, and so on.

The first option is preferred, but you can follow the second or third option if it suits your equipment set-up or it helps to accommodate a group of soldiers training at the same time.

- **UB/LB circuits—finding your starting load:** The proper load is the amount you can lift for that number of sets and reps and no more. For example, in sets of 15 reps, the weight should be what you can lift 15 times, but not quite 16 (this is sometimes called "15 RM" or "repetitions maximum"). You will have to experiment to find this load when you are just starting out. If you have been doing muscular strength and endurance work as a part of the EXPRES Programme you should have a good idea of the loads you can handle. If the load is too light for your first set, increase it for the second; if it's too heavy and you can't do all the reps, cut it back.

DOING IT ...

- **UB/LB circuits—increasing the load:** When you can do the required reps with a certain load comfortably on two successive training days, you should increase the load to keep your programme demanding. Add 5 kg for chest, back, and leg exercises, and 2 kg for arm exercises when adding weight. *Don't struggle with the loads.* Remember, when training do not go to failure on any set. Stop when you can still do one more rep before failure (this is called "Failure minus 1" or "F-1"). Record your sets, reps, and load for each exercise each session in your **Personal Training Record**. This can guide your efforts and make sure you get the most out of the programme.
- **Abdominal core exercises:** There are four abdominal core (AbCore) circuits included in Chapter 5. You will do *one* of them on each day they are included in the training routine. Start with Circuit #1 and do the sets, reps, and progression to the other circuits as noted there.

REMEMBER ...

> If you're doing a circuit using weights and find that the equipment you need isn't available (or you're uncomfortable using it), you can substitute the same numbered exercise in any of the other circuits as it will work the same muscle groups.

Power and Speed

The programme includes three elements: a **plyometric circuit**, **sprint programme**, and **field exercises**.

THE SET-UP

- The **plyometric circuit** is done at least once a week throughout the programme. Plyometrics involves exercises which rapidly stretch a muscle followed quickly by an explosive contraction of the same muscle. This is a very effective way to train for explosive power.
- The **sprint programme** is also done at least once a week throughout the 12-week routine. Moving your body weight at high speed repeatedly (with accompanying rest intervals) will improve your ability to move quickly during various soldiering activities.
- **Field exercises** enter the programme in Week 8. There is a casualty evacuation exercise (to simulate the casualty evacuation), an ammunition box lift exercise, and a shovelling drill. These are vigorous activities to get you ready for the specific tasks of the AFS.

DOING IT

- **Plyometric circuit:** Five drills are included in all. Do the drills in order (1, 2, 3...) and repeat the circuit *twice* in Week 4 and *three times* thereafter.
- **Sprint programme:** Four different sprint *sets* are included (e.g., Set 1 = 20 m + jog back x 12). Do the combination of sets noted for each session in the **Training Prescription** chart.
- **Field exercises:** Instructions for these appear at the end of Chapter 5. Do the exercises in the order shown in the **Training Prescription** chart. Use the loads noted for each session and complete the required number of reps and sets.

Optional Training Day

You'll note in the **Training Prescription** charts that Day 6 (Saturday) is listed as *Optional*. This day is for **you to do some extra training** where it may be needed.

Each day lists two workout options: One is continuous aerobic (plus an abdominal core circuit); the other is strength and power/speed training. To determine which one you should do:

- Look at your most recent fitness check results on your **Tracking Progress** chart. Compare your current levels for the *aerobic* and *strength* components.
- Choose the workout that covers the area where you are currently at the lower level. For example, if you are at Level 2 in aerobic and Level 1 in strength, do the strength and power/speed workout. If you are the same in both, do the aerobics/abdominal core workout— aerobics/AbCore is always the priority.
- Follow this selection procedure each **Optional Day** until you are at Level 3 in both these areas.
- If you are still below Level 3 in the **abdominal core** or **power/speed** components, continue to do the workout that includes those activities until they are at Level 3 as well.
- When everything is at Level 3, use the **Optional Day** for a sports activity, family activity, as an extra rest day if you feel you need it, or do the workout of your choice from the options provided.

Special Upper-Body Strength and Aerobics Circuit

This routine is ideal for all soldiers who need to improve *both* aerobic capacity and upper-body strength significantly. To perform this circuit:

- Ensure that there is a set of stairs nearby or set up a box stair (20-30 cm height) next to the weight-training equipment.
- Select one UB circuit and perform the sets/reps noted in the **Training Prescription** instructions for your current training week.
- Between each set, move quickly to the stairs or box and complete *one minute* of box stepping at a good pace.
- If you are using stack weights or free weights and have to wait for equipment to become available, continue box stepping during this time.

The idea is to keep moving throughout the workout so that your heart rate remains elevated the entire time. This is a great activity to include during optional training days.

BOX STEPPING...

Step up on to the box with the right foot, then bring the left foot up. Step down with the right foot, then step down with the left foot.

Repeat rapidly in succession. Alternate stepping up with the right foot then the left.

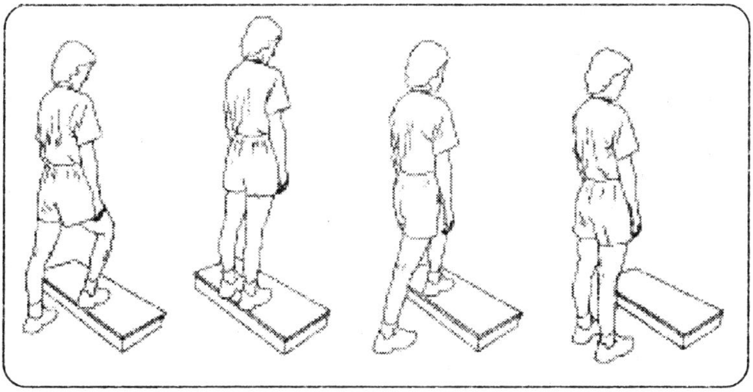

Fitness Maintenance

Once you have reached the level of fitness necessary to pass the AFS and completed your annual assessment, you will want to maintain a good fitness level throughout the year. There is no time for complacency. It is easier to *maintain* your fitness than to let it go and have to build back up again.

Fitness maintenance is possible with *three* good training sessions per week. You can complement these with other sports and recreational activities that you enjoy. For maintenance training:

- Do one strength session, one continuous aerobic session, and one interval aerobic session each week.
- Keep the intensity and duration of your aerobic sessions high enough to maintain Level 3 on the **Fitness Check** items.
- Test yourself using the nine **Fitness Check** items every few months to assess your programme. If you are not maintaining the necessary level of fitness, go back on the full programme.

There may be times when you can't follow the programme as outlined (if you are away from the base or on a course, for example). In most locations, you should be able to find a safe and convenient place to run, but indoor exercise on a stationary bicycle or rowing machine can keep you going until you get back to your regular programme. If strength-training equipment isn't available, the body-weight circuits can serve as your strength routine.

3

Training Prescriptions

This chapter contains the core information of the programme. You will turn to it *first* every training session to get your directions.

The **Training Prescription** charts outline exactly what you are to do each day. The sessions are designed so they can be completed within 60 minutes, with the exception of the weightload marches in the latter part of the programme. Each chart covers four weeks of training. Here's how to proceed:

- There are **Guidelines** on the page following each chart. Read these Guidelines from beginning to end *before* your first session in Weeks 1, 5, and 9.
- Note that the days are labelled Day 1 through Day 7 with corresponding Monday to Sunday included. There may be times when Day 1 cannot be on a Monday such as during field exercises or when adjustments are necessary to accommodate a large number of soldiers

at a base or other responsibilities in your own personal schedule. Double labelling allows for flexibility.

- Go to the box for the appropriate *Week* and *Day*. Review the activities you are to do. Return to the **Guidelines** to find the page numbers where the details of these activities—fitness checks, circuits, field exercises, etc.—appear. Go to the appropriate page for directions for that activity. Use the Active Rest/Sports Day for easy activities you enjoy.
- The training routines for aerobic intervals, continuous aerobic (distance runs), and weightload marches are fully outlined in the **Training Prescription** charts. Reread the **Training Principles/ Aerobics** background information in Chapter 2 if you are unsure of anything.
- Day 3 (Wednesday) is for an *Active Rest* or *Sports Day*. Use it to enjoy easy walking, gardening, biking with the family, or to pursue a favourite sports activity.
- Note the abbreviations used in the chart (like *AbCore* for abdominal core exercises and *UB circuits* for upper-body circuits). These short forms are used to keep the charts as simple as possible.

Components of Every Training Session

The information in the **Training Prescription** chart covers the workout part of each session. You will, of course, include a warm-up and cool-down each time as well. So here's the general flow every time you train:

DO	Consult...	Also Consult...
WARM-UP...	Warm-up/Cool-down Stretching	
WORKOUT...	Training Prescription Chart Weeks 1-4, 5-8 or 9-12	Fine Tuning Your Programme (Chapter 4) Strength Training Circuits (Chapter 5) Alternative Exercises (Chapter 5) Power and Speed Training (Chapter 5)
COOL-DOWN...	Warm-up/Cool-down Stretching	

REMEMBER...

> The Training Prescription charts outline exactly what you are to do each day. A thorough warm-up and cool-down are important components of every session.

Overview

There are five training days each week. Day 3 is an active rest day or sports day and Day 7 is a total rest day. The activities for each training day are noted here for handy reference. Full details are provided on the **Training Prescription** charts starting on the next page.

	DAY 1 MONDAY	DAY 2 TUESDAY	DAY 3 WEDNESDAY	DAY 4 THURSDAY	DAY 5 FRIDAY	DAY 6 SATURDAY	DAY 7 SUNDAY
WEEK 1 to 4	Aerobic Fitness & Strength Checks	Strength Check	ACTIVE REST or SPORTS DAY	Power Check	Aerobic Check	Day Off	REST
	Aerobic Intervals & Strength	Strength & Power		Strength & Power	Continuous Aerobic & Strength	Continuous Aerobic & Strength – *OR* – Strength & Power	
	Aerobic Intervals & Strength	Strength & Power		Strength & Power	Continuous Aerobic & Strength	Continuous Aerobic & Strength – *OR* – Strength	
	Aerobic Intervals & Strength	Strength & Power		Strength & Power	Continuous Aerobic & Strength	Continuous Aerobic & Strength – *OR* – Strength & Power	
WEEK 5 to 8	Aerobic Fitness & Strength Checks	Strength Check	ACTIVE REST or SPORTS DAY	Power Check	Aerobic Check	Day Off	REST
	Aerobic Intervals & Strength	Strength & Power		Strength & Power	Continuous Aerobic & Strength	Continuous Aerobic & Strength – *OR* – Strength & Power	
	Aerobic Intervals & Strength	Strength & Power		Strength & Power	Weightload March & Strength	Continuous Aerobic & Strength – *OR* – Strength & Power	
	Aerobic Intervals & Strength	Field Exercises		Strength & Power	Weightload March	Continuous Aerobic & Strength – *OR* – Strength & Power	

	DAY 1 MONDAY	DAY 2 TUESDAY	DAY 3 WEDNESDAY	DAY 4 THURSDAY	DAY 5 FRIDAY	DAY 6 SATURDAY	DAY 7 SUNDAY
WEEK 9 to 12	Aerobic Fitness & Strength Checks	Strength Check	ACTIVE REST or SPORTS DAY	Power Check	Aerobic Check	Day Off	REST
	Weightload March	Field Exercises		Strength & Power	Weightload March	Continuous Aerobic & Strength – *OR* – Strength & Power	
	Weightload March	Field Exercises		Strength & Power	Weightload March	Continuous Aerobic & Strength – *OR* – Strength & Power	
	Weightload March	Field Exercises		Strength & Power	Weightload March	Continuous Aerobic & Strength – *OR* – Strength & Power	

TRAINING PRESCRIPTION
for Weeks 1 to 4

	DAY 1 MONDAY	DAY 2 TUESDAY	DAY 3 WEDNESDAY	DAY 4 THURSDAY	DAY 5 FRIDAY	DAY 6 SATURDAY	DAY 7 SUNDAY
WEEK 1	Aerobic Fitness Check: 2400 m run Strength Check: push-ups	Strength Check: bench press, squats, sit-ups	ACTIVE REST or SPORTS DAY	Power Check: standing long-jump, 2-jump, 40 m sprint	Aerobic Check: 5 km run	DAY OFF	REST
WEEK 2	AEROBIC INTERVALS 1 min. work/ 1 min. easy x 12 STRENGTH AbCore: Choose one circuit	STRENGTH One UB Circuit, 2 sets of 15 RM One LB Circuit: 1 set of 15 RM POWER Sprint Programme Sets 1 and 2	ACTIVE REST or SPORTS DAY	STRENGTH One UB Circuit, 2 sets of 15 RM One LB Circuit: 1 set of 15 RM POWER Sprint Programme Sets 1 and 2	CONTINUOUS AEROBIC 34 min. "JT" STRENGTH AbCore: Choose one circuit	CONTINUOUS AEROBIC 34 min. "JT" STRENGTH AbCore: Choose one circuit — OR — STRENGTH One UB Circuit 2 sets x 15 RM POWER Sprint Programme Set 1 and Set 2	REST

	DAY 1 MONDAY	DAY 2 TUESDAY	DAY 3 WEDNESDAY	DAY 4 THURSDAY	DAY 5 FRIDAY	DAY 6 SATURDAY	DAY 7 SUNDAY
WEEK 3	AEROBIC INTERVALS 1 min. work / 1 min. easy x 15 STRENGTH AbCore: Choose one circuit	STRENGTH One UB Circuit, 2 sets of 12 RM One LB Circuit: 1 set of 15 RM POWER Sprint Programme Sets 1 and 2	ACTIVE REST or SPORTS DAY	STRENGTH One UB Circuit, 2 sets of 12RM POWER Sprint Programme Sets 1, 2 and 3	CONTINUOUS AEROBIC 38 min. "JT" STRENGTH AbCore: Choose one circuit	CONTINUOUS AEROBIC 38 min. "JT" STRENGTH AbCore: Choose one circuit — OR — STRENGTH One UB Circuit One LB Circuit 2 sets of 12 RM each exercise	REST
WEEK 4	AEROBIC INTERVALS 1 min. work/ 1 min. easy x 17 STRENGTH AbCore: Choose one circuit	STRENGTH One UB Circuit, 2 sets of 12 RM One LB Circuit: 1 set of 12 RM POWER Plyometric Circuit	ACTIVE REST or SPORTS DAY	STRENGTH One UB Circuit, One LB Circuit: 2 sets of 10 RM each exercise POWER Sprint Programme Set 3 Only	CONTINUOUS AEROBIC 42 min. "JT" STRENGTH AbCore: Choose one circuit	CONTINUOUS AEROBIC 42 min. "JT" STRENGTH AbCore: Choose one circuit — OR — STRENGTH One UB Circuit: 2 sets of 10 RM POWER Plyometric Circuit	REST

GUIDELINES

FITNESS CHECKS

Nine items are completed in Week 1. Instructions, the scoring table and record chart appear in Chapter 4.

AEROBIC INTERVALS (DAY 1)

Approximate *distance* you will cover for each one-minute work interval will depend on your level achieved in the 2400 m run/Aerobic Check in Week 1 as follows:

Level 1 - 200 m Level 2 - 225 m Level 3 - 250 m Level 4 - 275 m

CONTINUOUS AEROBIC (DAY 5)

Your approximate *"just talk"* or "JT" pace (in m/min) for your distance runs will depend on your level achieved in the 5 km run/Aerobic Check in Week 1 as follows:

Level 1 - 180 m/min Level 2 - 200 m/min Level 3 - 220 m/min Level 4 - 240 m/min

STRENGTH TRAINING

The Abdominal-Core (AbCore) exercises are done on Day 1, Day 5, and Day 6 (Optional). You can choose from any of the four circuits.

The Upper-Body (UB) exercise circuit is done on Day 2, Day 4 and Day 6 (Optional). Choose from the five circuits.

The Lower-Body (LB) exercise circuit is done on Day 2 and Day 4. Choose from the five circuits.

Set the load that allows you to do the sets and reps noted. Remember, when training do not go to failure on any set. Stop when you can still do one more rep before failure (this is called "Failure minus 1" or "F-1").

SPEED AND POWER TRAINING

The Plyometric circuit is done on Day 2 of Week 4 and sometimes on Day 6 (Optional).

The Sprint programme is done on Day 2 and 4 of Weeks 2 and 3, and Day 4 of Week 4 and sometimes on Day 6 (Optional).

DAY 6 — OPTIONAL

First priority is the Continuous Aerobic and Strength (AbCore) routine. Second priority is the Strength and Power routine.

	DAY 1 MONDAY	DAY 2 TUESDAY	DAY 3 WEDNESDAY	DAY 4 THURSDAY	DAY 5 FRIDAY	DAY 6 SATURDAY	DAY 7 SUNDAY
WEEK 5	Aerobic Fitness Check: 2400 m run Strength Check: push-ups	Strength Check: bench press, squats, sit-ups	ACTIVE REST or SPORTS DAY	Power Check: standing long-jump, 2-jump, 40 m sprint	Aerobic Check: 5 km run	DAY OFF	REST
WEEK 6	AEROBIC INTERVALS 2 min. work/ 2 min. easy x 6 STRENGTH AbCore: Choose one circuit	STRENGTH One UB Circuit, 2 sets of 15 RM One LB Circuit: 1 set of 15 RM POWER Sprint Programme Sets 1 and 2	ACTIVE REST or SPORTS DAY	STRENGTH One UB Circuit, 2 sets of 15 RM One LB Circuit: 1 set of 15 RM POWER Sprint Programme Sets 2 and 3	CONTINUOUS AEROBIC 40 min. "JT" STRENGTH AbCore: Choose one circuit	CONTINUOUS AEROBIC 40 min. "JT" STRENGTH AbCore: Choose one circuit — OR — STRENGTH One UB Circuit: 2 sets of 12 RM POWER Plyometric Circuit	REST

	DAY 1 MONDAY	DAY 2 TUESDAY	DAY 3 WEDNESDAY	DAY 4 THURSDAY	DAY 5 FRIDAY	DAY 6 SATURDAY	DAY 7 SUNDAY
WEEK 7	AEROBIC INTERVALS 2 min. work/ 2 min. easy x 7 STRENGTH AbCore: Choose one circuit	STRENGTH One UB Circuit, 2 sets of 12 RM One LB Circuit: 1 set of 12 RM POWER Plyometric Circuit	ACTIVE REST or SPORTS DAY	STRENGTH One UB Circuit, 2 sets of 12 RM One LB Circuit: 1 set of 12 RM POWER Sprint Programme Sets 3 and 4	WEIGHTLOAD MARCH 5 km with 15 kg pack (Time = 1 hr) Pace: 5 km/hr STRENGTH AbCore: Choose one circuit	CONTINUOUS AEROBIC 40 min. "JT" STRENGTH AbCore: Choose one circuit — OR — STRENGTH One UB Circuit: 2 sets of 12 RM and POWER Sprint Programme Sets 3 and 4	REST
WEEK 8	AEROBIC INTERVALS 2 min. work/ 2 min. easy x 8 STRENGTH AbCore: Choose one circuit	FIELD EXERCISES 4 sets each of: casualty evacuation 20 m out and back ammunition box lift/ lower x 20 reps shovel drill (20 full)	ACTIVE REST or SPORTS DAY	STRENGTH One UB Circuit, 1 set of 10 RM One LB Circuit: 1 set of 10 RM AbCore: One circuit POWER Sprint Programme Set 4	WEIGHTLOAD MARCH 8 km with 15 kg pack (Time = 1 hr 30 min, Pace = 5.33 km/hr)	CONTINUOUS AEROBIC 40 min. "JT" STRENGTH AbCore: Choose one circuit — OR — STRENGTH One UB Circuit: 2 sets of 10 RM POWER Plyometric Circuit	REST

Study the Guidelines for each activity on the next page...

GUIDELINES

FITNESS CHECKS

Nine items are completed in Week 5.

AEROBIC INTERVALS (DAY 1)

Approximate *distance* you will cover for each two-minute work interval will depend on your level achieved in the 2400 m run/Aerobic Check in Week 5 as follows:

Level 1 - 400 m Level 2 - 450 m
Level 3 - 500 m Level 4 - 550 m

CONTINUOUS AEROBIC (DAY 5)

Your approximate *"just talk"* or "JT" pace (in m/min) for your distance runs will depend on your level achieved in the 5 km run/Aerobic Check in Week 5 as follows:

Level 1 - 180 m/min Level 2 - 200 m/min

Level 3 - 220 m/min Level 4 - 240 m/min

FIELD EXERCISES (DAY 2)

These are done in Week 8. Instructions for the casualty evacuation, ammunition box lift/lower, and shovelling drill appear at the end of Chapter 5.

STRENGTH TRAINING

The Abdominal Core (AbCore) exercises are done on Day 1, Day 5, and

Day 6 (Optional). Choose one circuit.

The Upper-Body (UB) exercise circuit is done on Day 2, Day 4 and Day 6

(Optional). Choose one.

The Lower-Body (LB) exercise circuit is done on Day 2 and Day 4. Choose one.

Set the load that allows you to do the sets and reps noted. Remember, when training do not go to failure on any set. Stop when you can still do one more rep before failure (this is called "Failure minus 1" or "F-1").

SPEED AND POWER TRAINING

The Plyometric circuit is done on Day 2 of Week 7 and sometimes on Day 6 (Optional).

The Sprint programme is done on Day 2 and 4 of Week 6, and Day 4 of Weeks 7 and 8 and sometimes on Day 6 (Optional).

DAY 6 — OPTIONAL

First priority is the Continuous Aerobic and Strength (AbCore) routine. Second priority is the Strength and Power routine.

	DAY 1 MONDAY	DAY 2 TUESDAY	DAY 3 WEDNESDAY	DAY 4 THURSDAY	DAY 5 FRIDAY	DAY 6 SATURDAY	DAY 7 SUNDAY
WEEK 9	Aerobic Fitness Check: 2400 m run Strength Check: push-ups	Strength Check: bench press, squats, sit-ups	ACTIVE REST or SPORTS DAY	Power Check: standing long-jump, 2-jump, 40 m sprint	Aerobic Check: 5 km run	DAY OFF	REST
WEEK 10	WEIGHTLOAD MARCH 7.5 km with 20 kg pack (Time = 1 hr 30 min, Pace = 5 km/hr)	FIELD EXERCISES 5 sets each of: casualty evacuation 20 m out and back ammunition box lift/ lower x 20 reps shovel drill (20 full)	ACTIVE REST or SPORTS DAY	STRENGTH UB Circuit #3: 2 sets of 12 RM POWER Sprints: 4 x 20 m every 10 sec 3 x 40 m every 20 sec 2 x 60 m every 30 sec	WEIGHTLOAD MARCH 8 km with 24.5 kg pack (Time = 1 hr 30 min, Pace = 5.33 km/hr)	CONTINUOUS AEROBIC 40 min. "JT" STRENGTH AbCore: Choose one circuit — OR — STRENGTH One UB Circuit: 2 sets of 12 RM POWER Plyometric Circuit	REST

	DAY 1 MONDAY	DAY 2 TUESDAY	DAY 3 WEDNESDAY	DAY 4 THURSDAY	DAY 5 FRIDAY	DAY 6 SATURDAY	DAY 7 SUNDAY
WEEK 11	WEIGHTLOAD MARCH 8 km with 24.5 kg pack (Time = 1 hr 20 min, Pace = 6.0 km/hr)	FIELD EXERCISES 4 sets each of: casualty evacuation 30 m out and back ammunition box lift/ lower x 30 reps shovel drill (30 full)	ACTIVE REST or SPORTS DAY	STRENGTH UB Circuit #3: 2 sets of 10 RM POWER Sprints: 6 x 20 m every 10 sec 4 x 40 m every 20 sec 2 x 60 m every 30 sec	WEIGHTLOAD MARCH 10 km with 24.5 kg pack (Time = 1 hr 50 min, Pace = 5.5 km/hr)	CONTINUOUS AEROBIC 40 min. "JT" STRENGTH AbCore: Choose one circuit — OR — STRENGTH One UB Circuit: 2 sets of 10 RM POWER Sprint Programme Set 4	REST
WEEK 12	WEIGHTLOAD MARCH 10 km with 24.5 kg pack (Time = 1 hr 40 min, Pace = 6 km/hr)	FIELD EXERCISES 3 sets each of: casualty evacuation 40 m out and back ammunition box lift/ lower x 40 reps shovel drill (40 full)	ACTIVE REST or SPORTS DAY	STRENGTH UB Circuit #3: 2 sets of 15 RM POWER Sprints: 4 x 20 m every 30 sec 3 x 40 m every 20 sec 2 x 60 m every 10 sec	WEIGHTLOAD MARCH 13 km with 24.5 kg pack (Time = 2 hr 26 min 20 sec, Pace = 5.33 km/hr)	CONTINUOUS AEROBIC 40 min. "JT" STRENGTH AbCore: Choose one circuit — OR — STRENGTH One UB Circuit: 2 sets of 15 RM POWER Plyometric Circuit	REST

Study the Guidelines for each activity on the next page...

GUIDELINES

FITNESS CHECKS

Nine items are completed in Week 9.

WEIGHTLOAD MARCH (DAYS 1 AND 5)

In Weeks 11 and 12, these are done in full fighting order, including combat clothes, helmet, weapon, and rucksac (weight is total kit: ie., weapon, EIS, helmet, webbing and field pack). The *distance* and *time* for each march is noted (equating to a specific pace).

FIELD EXERCISES (DAY 2)

These are done in Weeks 10, 11, and 12.

STRENGTH TRAINING

The Abdominal Core (AbCore) exercises are done on Day 6 (Optional). Choose one circuit.

The Upper-Body (UB) exercise circuit is done on Day 4 and Day 6 (Optional). Choose one circuit.

Set the load that allows you to do the sets and reps noted. Remember, when training do not go to failure on any set. Stop when you can still do one more rep before failure (this is called "Failure minus 1" or "F-1").

SPEED AND POWER TRAINING

The Plyometric circuit is done on Day 6 (Optional). Sprint programme sets are done on Day 6 (Optional). A special sprint routine is done on Day 4, Weeks 10-12.

DAY 6 — OPTIONAL

First priority is the Continuous Aerobic and Strength (AbCore) routine. Second priority is the Strength and Power routine.

4

Fine Tuning Your Programme

Nine fitness items are included to help you establish the starting point in your programme and check your progress along the way:

- two for **aerobic fitness**—2400 m and 5 km runs
- four for **strength**—bench press, push-ups, squats, and sit-ups
- three for **power**—standing long jump, 2-jump, and 40-m sprint.

You are to check your status in these areas during Weeks 1, 5, and 9 (on the days shown in the **Training Prescription** charts).

- Use the descriptions and illustrations in this chapter as a guide to be sure you do things correctly.
- Use whichever loads suit you for the Bench Press and Squat items. Don't worry if you are unable to do the

heaviest load for each of these. Remember that smaller people have smaller muscle mass and simply may not be able to attain the strength required to lift these heavy loads. It may mean that when you are doing the Ammunition Box Lift you are working closer to your full strength, but with proper training you should still be able to reach the required standard.

- If you are unaccustomed to any of the more dynamic items (such as the 40-metre sprint), you can exclude these from the Week 1 check. Begin your training, then do them for the first time in Week 5.

Use the **Fitness Check** table provided to determine your *level* in each of the nine items. Record these in the **Tracking Progress** chart on the page following the table. Note your specific score (time, reps, or distance) for each item. This progress chart makes it easy for you to see how you are doing, showing *gains* as you improve your time, reps, or distance and *major steps* forward as you move from one level to the next.

Achieving Level 1 in the **Fitness Check** is roughly equivalent to achieving CFMPFS. You should aim for Level 3 to give you the reserve to do all four AFS tasks.

EASY AS 1, 2, 3...

Monitoring your progress :

1. Complete the nine Fitness Check items.
2. Locate your level son the Fitness Check table.
3. Record your score sand levels on your Tracking Progress chart.

THE FITNESS CHECK

Checking Your Aerobic Fitness

2400 Metre Run : This is six laps of a 400 metre track. Pace yourself well. Don't start out *too* quickly! Do an easy jog and stretching warm-up prior to the run. Rest 15 minutes on completion of the run, then repeat it. Use the first run to go for your best time; use the second one as a training run.

5 Kilometre Run: This is a timed run over a measured course *or* 12½ laps of a 400-metre track. As with the 2400 m run, pace yourself and don't be too enthusiastic at first. Warm-up thoroughly prior to the run.

Checking Your Strength

Bench Press: Feet flat on the floor, back flat on the bench, and a secure grip on the bar with the hands a comfortable distance apart. Try one repetition with 55 kg. If you do it comfortably, continue and do as many repetitions as you can. If you struggle to do one rep at 55 kg, drop down to 45 kg to do your **Fitness Check** this time.

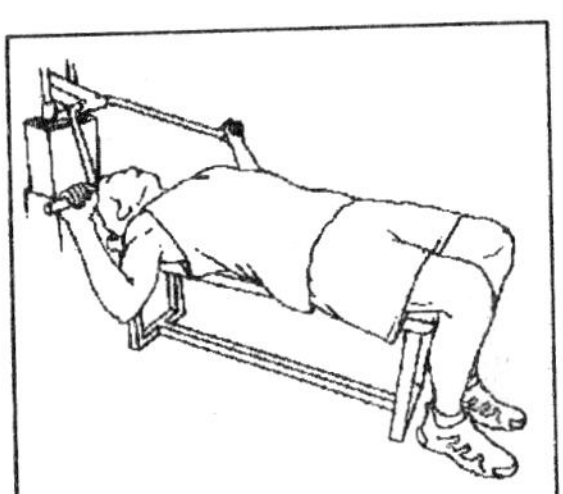

- If you use 55 kg and do 11 reps or less, use 45 kg for your *next* **Fitness Check**. If you do 22 or more reps, use 65 kg *next time.*
- If you use 45 kg for your **Fitness Check** and do 11 reps or less, use 45 kg again *next time.*

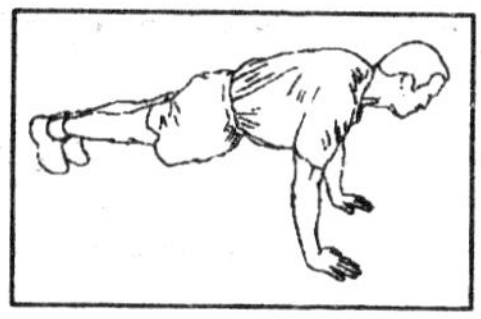

Push-ups: Do push-ups at a rate of 25 per minute for a maximum of 45 repetitions (use a metronome or count for timing). Place your hands shoulder-width apart, fingers pointing forward, and keep your back straight. Lower until you have a 90° bend at the elbows.

Squats : Use a squat rack and barbell. With feet shoulder width apart, toes pointing slightly outward, back erect, and barbell on the shoulders, squat to a 90° bend at the knees then return to full extension. Try one repetition with 70 kg. If you do it comfortably, continue and do as many repetitions as you can. If you struggle to do one rep at 70 kg, drop down to 60 kg to do your **Fitness Check** this time.

- If you use 70 kg and do 11 reps or less, use 60 kg for your *next* **Fitness Check**. If you do 22 or more reps, use 80 kg *next time.*
- If you use 60 kg for your **Fitness Check** and do 11 reps or less, use 60 kg again *next time.*

Sit-ups: Do sit-ups at the rate of 25 per minute to a maximum of 100 repetitions. With your knees bent and feet held down, curl up to touch your elbows to your knees.

Checking Your Power

Standing Long Jump: Record the maximum distance jumped in your best of three attempts. Measure from your toes on the starting line to where your heels land. Use a full arm swing and bend your legs to get a good push off.

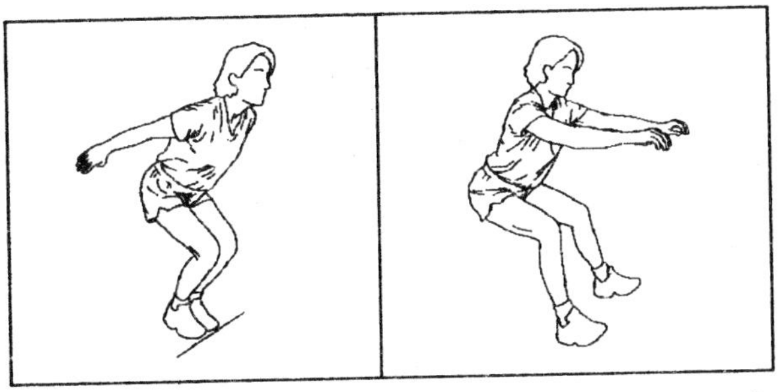

2-Jump: Record the maximum distance jumped in your best of three attempts. Measure from your toes on the starting line to your heel on final landing. Start with one foot on the start line, jump to the other foot then to the starting foot without pausing. Use your arms to drive you forward during the jump.

40-Metre Sprint: Record your best time of two attempts. Place one foot ahead of the other at the start. Lean forward and drive your arms to get moving.

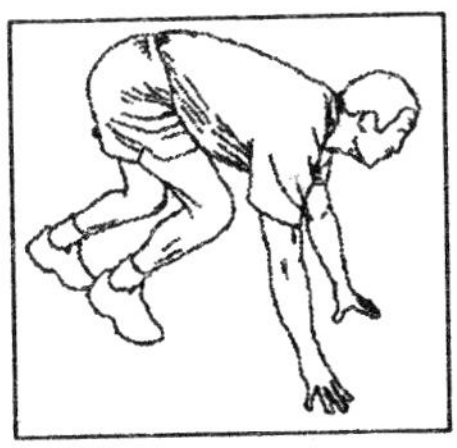

Fitness Check

Use this table to determine your *level* in each of the nine items:

FITNESS ITEMS	GETTING STARTED	Level 1	Level 2	Level 3*	Level 4
AEROBIC					
2400 m Run Standard	>13:15 min:s	13:15-11:46 min:s	11:45-10:31 min:s	10:30-9:16 min:s	<9:16 min:s
5 km Run Standard	>29:00 min:s	29:00-27:01 min:s	27:00-25:01 min:s	25:00-23:01 min:s	<23:00 min:s
STRENGTH Upper Body Bench Press Standard					
65 kg (approx. 145 lb)	<9 reps	9-13 reps	14-17 reps	18-21 reps	22+ reps
55 kg (approx. 120 lb)	<11 reps	11-16 reps	17-21 reps	22-27 reps	28+ reps
45 kg (approx. 100 lb)	<14 reps	14-20 reps	21-26 reps	27-32 reps	33+ reps
Push-Ups Standard	<20 reps	20-29 reps	30-39 reps	40-44 reps	45+ reps
Lower Body Squats Standard					
80 kg (approx. 175 lb)	<5 reps	5-8 reps	9-11 reps	12-14 reps	15+ reps
70 kg (approx. 155 lb)	<6 reps	6-9 reps	10-13 reps	14-17 reps	18+ reps
60 kg (approx. 135 lb)	<7 reps	7-11 reps	12-16 reps	17-20 reps	21+ reps
Abdominal Core					
Sit-ups Standard	<20 reps	20-44 reps	45-74 reps	75-99 reps	100+ reps
POWER AND SPEED					
Long Jump Standard	<200 cm	200-229 cm	230-249 cm	250-274 cm	275+ cm
Two-Jump Standard	<325 cm	325-374 cm	375-449 cm	450-499 cm	500+ cm
40 m Sprint Standard	>6.20 s	6.20-5.91 s	5.90-5.61 s	5.60-5.31 s	<5.3 s

Record your score (time/reps/distance) and level for each item on the next page...

*It is recommended that you aim to achieve Level 3 to give you the reserve to do all four tasks of the AFS.

Tracking Progress

Record your *score* (time/reps/distance) and *level* for each item:

FITNESS ITEMS	Week 1		Week 5		Week 9	
	SCORE	LEVEL	SCORE	LEVEL	SCORE	LEVEL
AEROBIC 2400 m Run (min/s)						
5 km Run (min/s)						
STRENGTH Upper Body Bench Press 65 kg (approx. 145 lb)						
55 kg (approx. 120 lb)						
45 kg (approx. 100 lb)						
Push-Ups						
Lower Body Squats 80 kg (approx. 175 lb)						
70 kg (approx. 155 lb)						
60 kg (approx. 135 lb)						
Abdominal Core Sit-Ups						
POWER AND SPEED Long Jump						
Two-Jump						
40 m Sprint						

5

Training Circuits and Routines

This chapter provides detailed descriptions of exercises and activities you will perform during your training. On any given Week and Day of your programme, the **Training Prescription** chart will refer you to specific information here.

The chapter is organized in five sections:

- a warm-up and cool-down stretching routine
- strength-training circuits (for the upper body, lower body, and abdominal core)
- alternative exercises using equipment such as beams, ropes, and logs
- power and speed training routines, including a plyometric circuit, a sprint programme and field exercises. The field exercises simulate the AFS tasks.

Warm-up and Stretching

The warm-up is important prior to each training session. It reduces your risk of injury and it gets you physically and mentally prepared to train. A good warm-up:

- reduces the stiffness in muscles to increase efficiency
- improves blood flow to muscles to increase the delivery of oxygen, fuels, and hormones, to help remove waste products, and to assist in heat loss
- allows for faster nerve impulses
- can reduce the risk of soft-tissue injuries.

A proper warm-up consists of three components:

- general warm-up ~ light aerobic activity
- static stretching
- specific warm-up.

You can do the light aerobic activity and stretching in whichever order your prefer, but always do the specific warm-up last. Here are some guidelines for each component:

General Warm-up

- Do light aerobic activity using large muscle groups such as jogging, marching or cycling.
- Spend 3-5 minutes on this.

Stretching

- On each exercise, stretch *slowly* to the end of your range of motion and hold for a minimum of 10 seconds at the beginning. Increase this to 20 second holds when you are accustomed to the exercises. Repeat 2-3 times.

- When exercises are done stretching one leg at a time, to one side, etc., repeat alternately to the other side.
- Stretch to the end of range of motion until you feel a tightness. If you feel pain, you are stretching too far.
- Inhale and exhale on each repetition, exhaling strongly as you initiate the stretch. Don't hold your breath.
- Spend 8-10 minutes on this. Don't rush.

Specific Warm-up

- Do a 1-3 minutes *specific* warm-up by gradually increasing the intensity of exercise *using the muscle groups that will be* used during the training session.
- When doing resistance training, for example, use the first set or first few reps of each exercise as a warm-up by keeping the load low and focusing on technique.
- When doing aerobic interval or continuous training or for sprint and plyometric work, use the specific exercise and gradually increase the intensity until you reach the training load.
- Spend 1-3 minutes on this part of the overall warm up. It will tune-up your nervous system and enhance performance in the early stages of the session.

Cool-down

At the end of each session do **cool-down** stretching for another 5 minutes. Return to the exercises that stretch the muscles most used during the session.

Stretching Sequence

1 Overhead Stretch

Inter lock your fingers above your head, straighten your arm sand stretch them up and slightly back.

2 Side Stretch

Reach one arm overhead and the other down the side of the leg.

3 Sit-Reach

One leg straight, one bent with sole of the foot near knee of straight leg. Reach out along straight leg.

4 Groin Stretch

Relax with your knees bent and soles of your feet together for a comfortable stretch. For an added stretch, put *gentle* pressure on the insides of your knees with your hands.

5 Low-Back Stretch

Pull one knee toward your chest by grasping the back of the thigh with your hands. Keep the back of your head touching the floor.

6 Leg Crossover

Place one bent leg across the other, stretching it toward the floor with gentle pressure from the opposite hand. Look in the other direction toward your out-stretched arm.

7 Lunge

Crouch over your bent front leg with the knee directly above the ankle. Place the knee of the back leg on the floor, then gently press the hip downward.

8 Thigh Stretch

Bend one knee, grasp the ankle, and pull your heel gently toward the buttock. Place your other hand on a wall for balance if you like, and don't arch your back.

9 Calf Stretch

One foot in front of the other and feet pointing straight ahead. Rock forward toward a wall bending the front leg to stretch the calf muscle of the back (straight) leg. Repeat with legs closer together and squatting to stretch the soleus muscle lower in the back leg.

10 Split Stretch

With your legs apart, feet pointing straight ahead, shift weight over one leg, keeping the other leg straight and both feet flat on the floor.

REMEMBER...

At the end of each session, to cool- down, return to the exercises that stretch the muscles most used during the session you have just completed.

STRENGTH-TRAINING CIRCUITS

There are fourteen circuits included here:

- five for **upper-body (UB)** strength
- five for **lower-body (LB)** strength
- four for **abdominal-core (AbCore)** strength.

Do the circuits on the required days as set out in the **Training Prescription** charts. Here are a few reminders:

- Whenever *stack weights* or *free weights* are available, do the circuits using them (UB and LB 1, 2, or 3) as much as possible. With the weights, you can control the load effectively and make good progress.

- If equipment or a weight you need isn't available or it feels uncomfortable doing a particular exercise, you can *substitute* the same numbered exercise from any of the other circuits (e.g., #1 in Circuit 4 for #1 in Circuit 2).
- When doing body-weight circuits do repetitions to the repetitions maximum (RM) noted. Don't struggle. Stop when you feel you could do just one more. (If you find the RM too easy for any of these exercises, you can add a few more repetitions or slow down the tempo.) For partner resistance circuits, work together giving each other feedback so the resistance (load) is at the right level.
- Breathe comfortably when doing the exercises. Inhale and exhale on each repetition, exhaling on effort.
- Use the illustrations and descriptions for each exercise as a guide to make sure you use the right technique. For exercises done in a standing position, the feet should be shoulder-width apart for good balance with the toes pointing slightly outward.
- When using stack weights or a barbell, hold the bar with the thumbs facing in toward one another unless noted otherwise. If the bar should be held with the thumbs facing out, this will be stated in the exercise description.
- Work with a partner. You can spot one another and provide technique guidance and encouragement. This is especially important for safety on free-weight exercises like bench press and squats.

- Do not sacrifice proper technique in order to increase the training load.

UPPER-BODY CIRCUIT #1

Using Stack Weights

If equipment or a weight you need isn't available or it feels uncomfortable doing a particular exercise, you can substitute the same number exercise from any of the other circuits.

1. BENCH PRESS

Lying flat on the bench, grasp the bar in a secure grip with your hands a comfortable distance apart, then press it to arms' length above the chest.

2. LAT PULL-DOWNS

Seated on a bench (or kneeling), pull the bar down in front of your face to shoulder level.

3. BACK EXTENSIONS

With your feet secured, hang your upper body down over the end of a bench with the hands clasped behind the head. Raise your upper body until parallel with the floor.

4. SHOULDER PRESS

Seated, push the bar up from shoulder height until your arms are fully extended overhead.

5. TRICEP EXTENSIONS

Hands close together and elbows bent 90°, push hands down until your arms are straight.

6. BICEP CURLS

Arms down in front and fully extended, grasping the bar with your thumbs facing out. Curl the bar, pulling your hands up under your chin.

1. BENCH PRESS

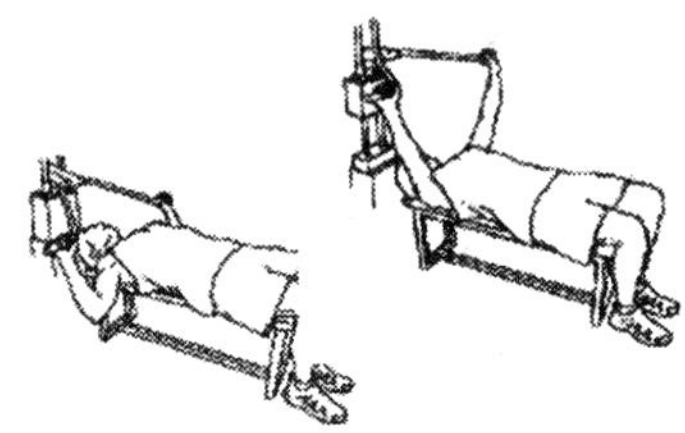

2. LAT PULL-DOWNS

3. BACK EXTENSIONS

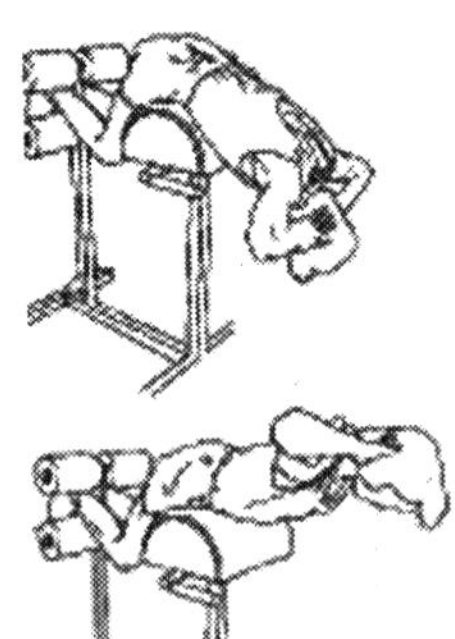

4. SHOULDER PRESS

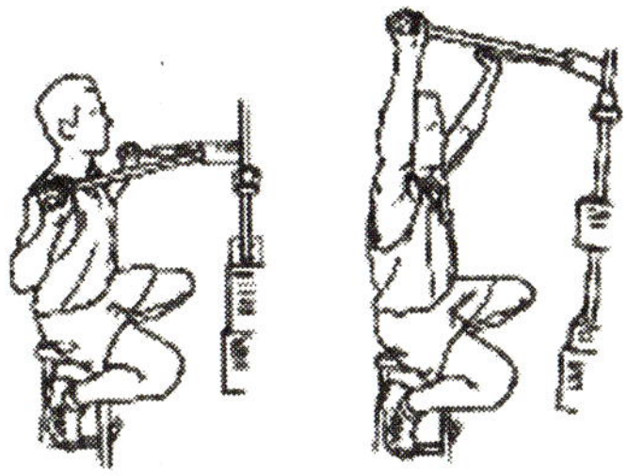

5. TRICEP EXTENSIONS

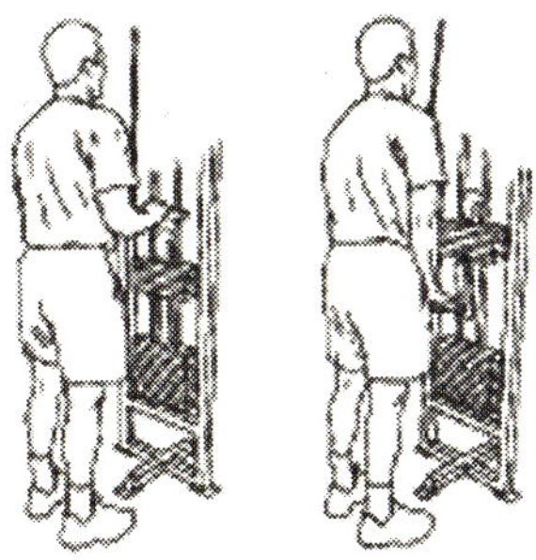

6. BICEP CURLS

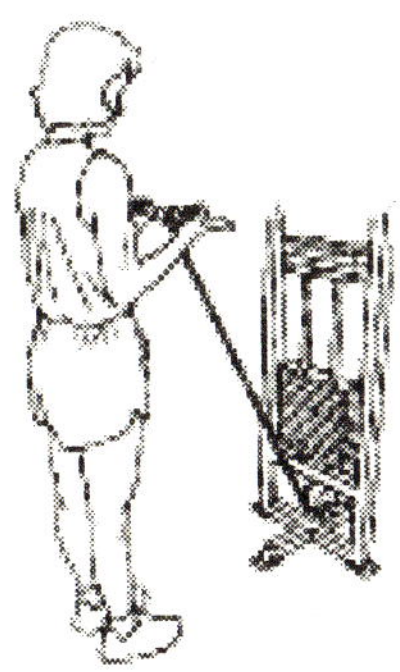

UPPER-BODY CIRCUIT #2

Using Free Weights (Barbell)

If equipment or a weight you need isn't available or it feels uncomfortable doing a particular exercise, you can substitute the same number exercise from any of the other circuits.

1. BENCH PRESS

Lying flat on the bench, grasp the bar in a secure grip with your hands a comfortable distance apart, then press it to arms' length above the chest.

2. BENT-OVER ROW

Standing and bent forward with a slight bend in the knees and arms extended below, pull the barbell into your abdomen keeping your elbows close to your sides. Keep your back flat.

3. DEAD LIFT

Grasp the barbell in front with your arms extended and your legs bent, straighten your legs to assume an upright standing position.

4. MILITARY PRESS

Seated with your arms bent in front and the barbell supported at shoulder height, push it to full extension overhead.

5. TRICEP EXTENSIONS

Seated with the barbell supported behind your neck, press the bar to full extension overhead. Keep elbows close to your head.

6. BICEP CURLS

Standing with your arms extended below in front and grasping the barbell, curl it up to shoulder height then curl it back down.

Note: Exercises 4 and 5 can also be done in a standing position. Work with a partner on these two exercises (and #1), spotting each other for safety.

1. BENCH PRESS

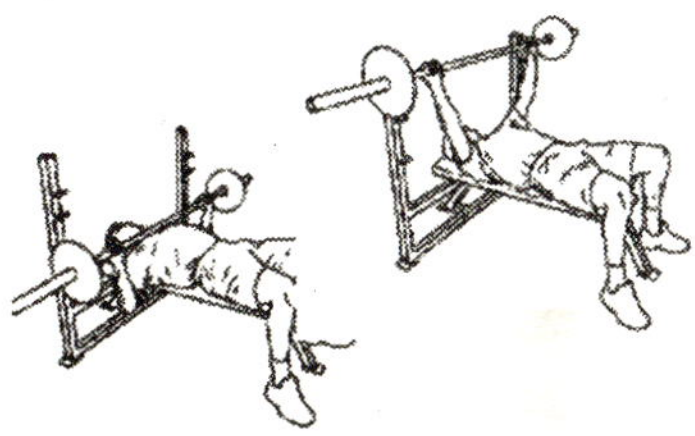

2. BENT-OVER ROW

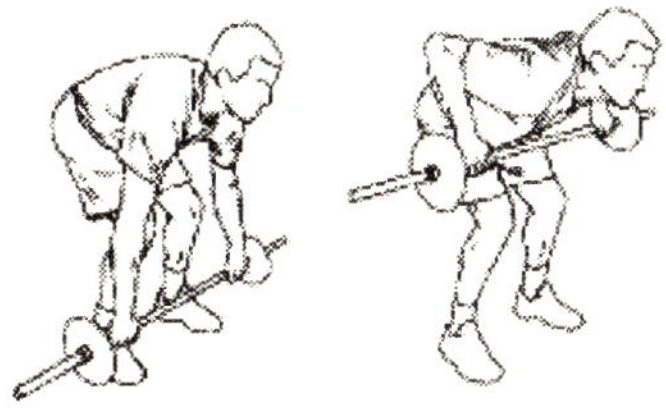

3. DEAD LIFT

4. MILITARY PRESS

5. TRICEP EXTENSIONS

6. BICEP CURLS

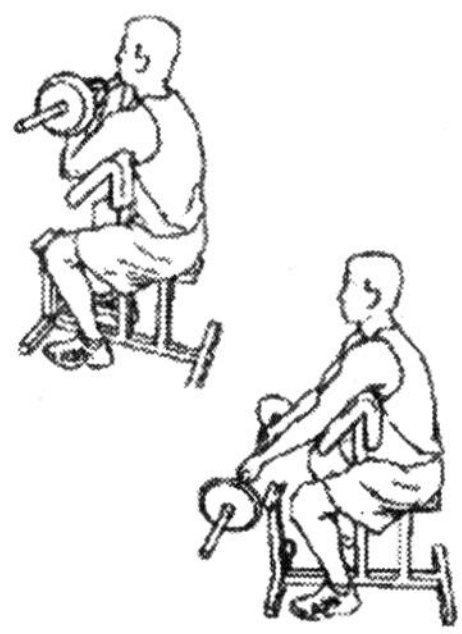

UPPER-BODY CIRCUIT #3

Using Free Weights (Dumbbells)

If equipment or a weight you need isn't available or it feels uncomfortable doing a particular exercise, you can substitute the same number exercise from any of the other circuits.

1. BENCH PRESS

Lying flat on the bench, grasp the dumbbells above your shoulders with your thumbs facing in, then press them to arms' length above your chest.

2. BENT-OVER DUMBBELL ROW

Standing and bent forward with a slight bend in your knees and arms extended below grasping dumbbells, pull them into your abdomen keeping elbows close to your sides. Keep your back flat.

3. DEAD LIFT

Bent forward with your knees slightly bent and grasping the dumbbells at your sides with arms extended, lift your upper body to return to an upright standing position.

4. SEATED PRESS

Holding the dumbbells at shoulder height, straighten your arms pressing the dumbbells to full arm extension overhead.

5. TRICEP EXTENSIONS

Holding one dumbbell overhead with both hands, bend your elbows to lower the weight behind your head then return to full arm extension.

6. BICEP CURLS

Sitting on a bench with your arms extended below and at your sides grasping the dumbbells. Curl one dumbbell up to shoulder height then curl it back down. Do alternately with the other arm.

Note: Exercises 4 and 5 can also be done in a standing position. Work with a partner on these two exercises (and #1), spotting each other for safety.

1. BENCH PRESS

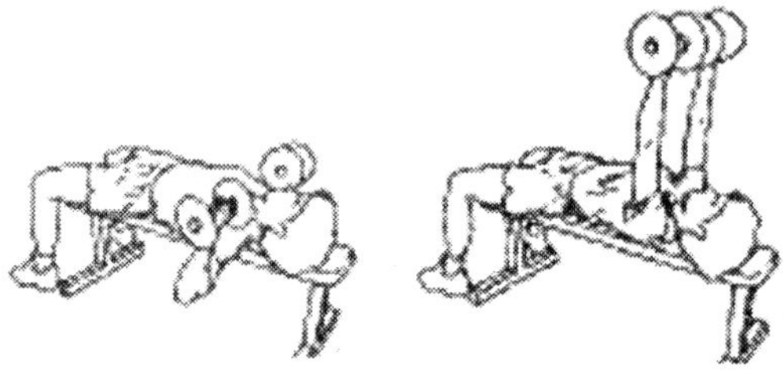

2. BENT-OVER DUMBBELL ROW

3. DEAD LIFT

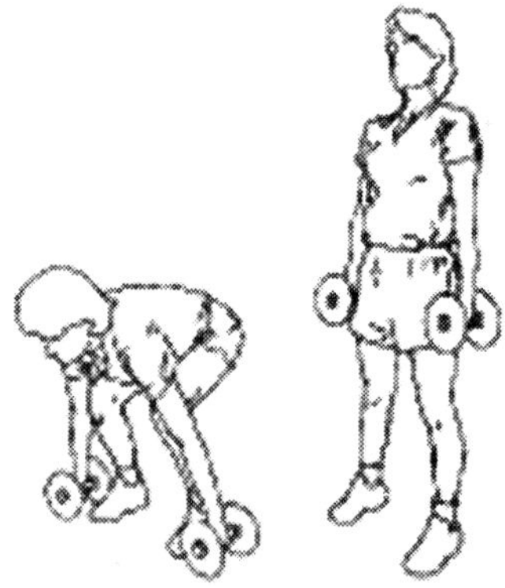

4. SEATED PRESS

5. TRICEP EXTENSIONS

6. BICEP CURLS

UPPER-BODY CIRCUIT #4

Body-Weight Exercises

If equipment or a weight you need isn't available or it feels uncomfortable doing a particular exercise, you can substitute the same number exercise from any of the other circuits.

1. PUSH-UPS (FINGERS FORWARD)

With the body held straight, push up, straightening your arms.

2. CHIN-UPS (HANDS OVER)

With your hands shoulder-width apart, pull up until your chin reaches the bar. Inhale as you pull up, exhale on the way back down.

3. BACK EXTENSIONS

With your feet secured, hang your upper body down over the end of a bench with your hands clasped behind your head. Raise your upper body until parallel with the floor.

4. PUSH-UPS (HANDS WIDE)

With your body held straight and hands out wide (more than shoulder width apart), push up straightening your arms.

5. DIPS

With your palms supported on a chair or bench behind your back, extend your arms until they are straight.

6. CHIN-UPS (HANDS UNDER)

With your hands shoulder-width apart and your thumbs facing out, pull up until your chin reaches the bar. Exhale as you pull up, inhale on the way back down.

Note: For Exercises 2 and 6, if you are unable to do a single chin-up at first, perform what are called "negatives". Use a box or a chair to help you get your chin level with the bar, then slowly lower yourself until your arms are straight. Try to pull yourself back up, then use the box to get back up to bar level and repeat. Alternatively, your partner can support some of your weight during the pull-up phase.

1. PUSH-UPS (FINGERS FORWARD)

2. CHIN-UPS (HANDS OVER)

3. BACK EXTENSIONS

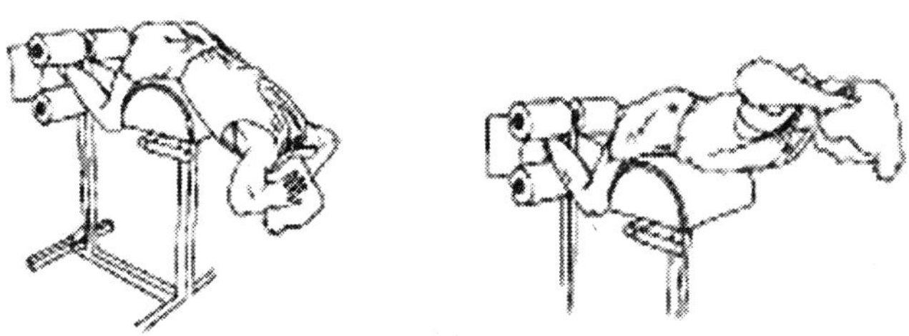

4. PUSH-UPS (HANDS WIDE)

5. DIPS

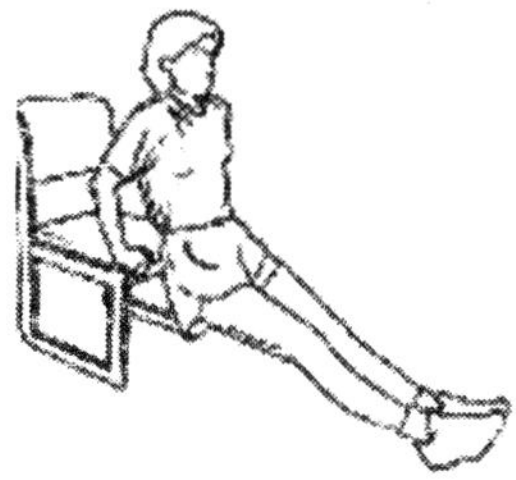

6. CHIN-UPS (HANDS UNDER)

UPPER-BODY CIRCUIT #5

Partner-Resistance Exercises

If equipment or a weight you need isn't available or it feels uncomfortable doing a particular exercise, you can substitute the same number exercise from any of the other circuits.

1. BENCH PRESS AND 2. BENT-OVER ROW

Soldier A does bench press (pushing the bar upward *and* pulling it downward) while Soldier B resists, then Soldier B does a bent-over row (pulling the bar upward *and* pushing it downward) while Soldier A resists. Switch roles and repeat. The standing soldier should keep his/her back flat.

3. SHOULDER PRESS AND 4. LAT PULL DOWN

Soldier A in front pushes bar upward to full arm extension while Soldier B resists downward, then Soldier B pulls bar back downward while Soldier A resists upward. Switch roles and repeat.

5. BICEP CURLS AND 6. TRICEP EXTENSIONS

Soldier A curls his/her arms upward while Soldier B resists, then Soldier B extends his/her arms downward while Soldier A resists. Switch roles and repeat.

Note: Do each of these exercises in a slow, controlled movement. When working with a partner, give each other feedback on technique, proper resistance, etc.

1. BENCH PRESS AND 2. BENT-OVER ROW

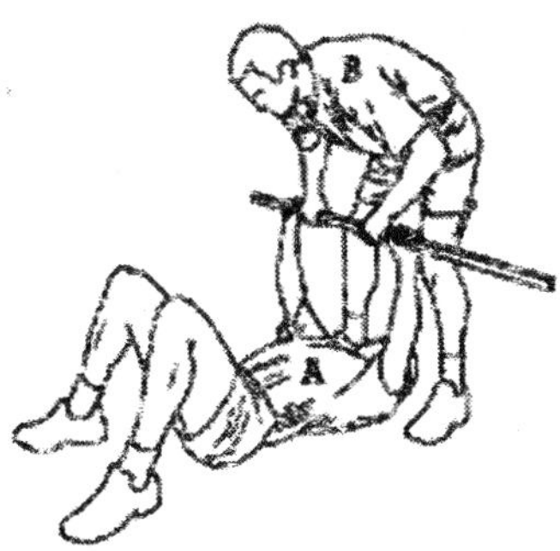

3. SHOULDER PRESS AND 4. LAT PULL DOWN

5. BICEP CURLS AND 6. TRICEP EXTENSIONS

LOWER-BODY CIRCUIT #1

Using Stack Weights

If equipment or a weight you need isn't available or it feels uncomfortable doing a particular exercise, you can substitute the same number exercise from any of the other circuits.

1. LEG PRESS

Set seat for a 90° bend at the knees and with the insteps on the pedals, push the pedals away extending the legs fully. (Can also do single-leg press.)

2. HAMSTRING CURLS

With your kneecaps just past the end of the bench, flex your knees, pulling your heels toward your buttocks.

3. CALF EXTENSIONS

With your insteps on the pedals and legs straight, push pedals away from you with your toes.

4. QUAD EXTENSIONS

With your shins behind the padded movement bar, extend your knees to straighten your legs in front.

5. HIP ADDUCTION

With the loop just below your knee on the leg farthest away from the pulley, draw that leg up and away.

1. LEG PRESS

2. HAMSTRING CURLS

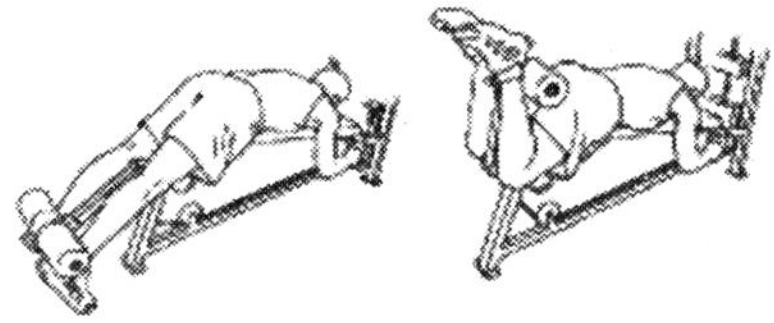

3. CALF EXTENSIONS

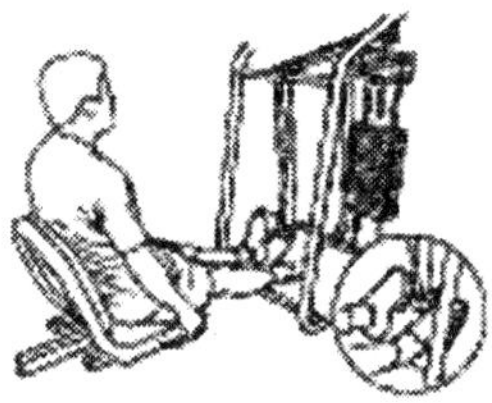

4. QUAD EXTENSIONS

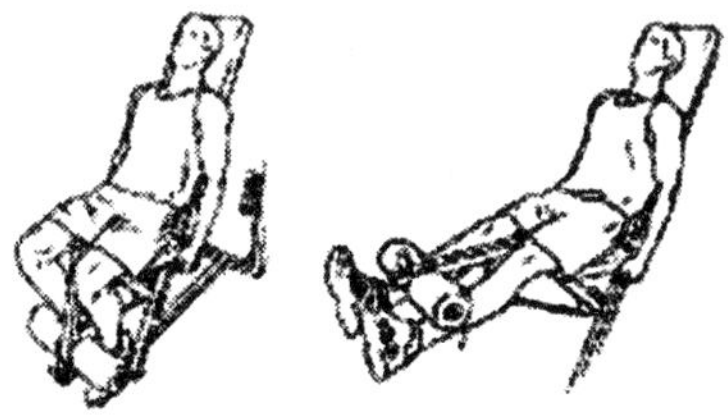

5. HIP ADDUCTION

LOWER-BODY CIRCUIT #2

Using Free Weights (Barbell, etc.)

If equipment or a weight you need isn't available or it feels uncomfortable doing a particular exercise, you can substitute the same number exercise from any of the other circuits.

1. BARBELL SQUATS

Standing erect, with your feet shoulder-width apart, your toes pointing slightly outward, and the barbell held on shoulders, bend your legs to squat (no lower than thighs parallel with the floor) then return to full standing position.

2. HAMSTRING CURLS

Lying face down on the floor with the knees just supported at the end of the bench, bend the knees, curling the heels toward the seat with partner resistance.

3. CALF RAISES

With your forefeet supported on a low board and a barbell held securely on your shoulders, raise up on your toes then slowly lower heels to the floor.

4. LUNGE SQUATS

Using a barbell or dumbbells, step forward with one foot, dropping your knee toward the floor and lifting your back heel off the floor. Alternate legs.

5. HIP ADDUCTION

Standing side on to a wall or bench for balance and using an ankle weight or tubing, draw your outside leg inward and across in front of the other.

6. HIP ABDUCTION

Standing side on to a wall or bench for balance and using an ankle weight or tubing, draw your outside leg up and away.

1. BARBELL SQUATS

2. HAMSTRING CURLS 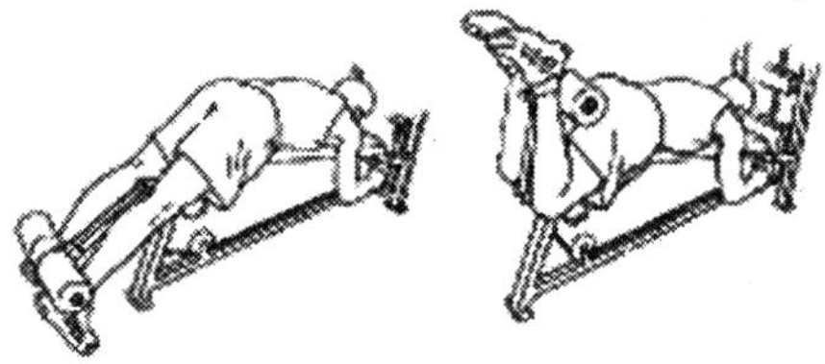
3. CALF RAISES 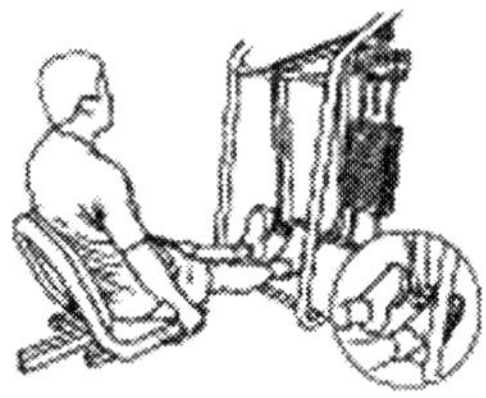
4. LUNGE SQUATS 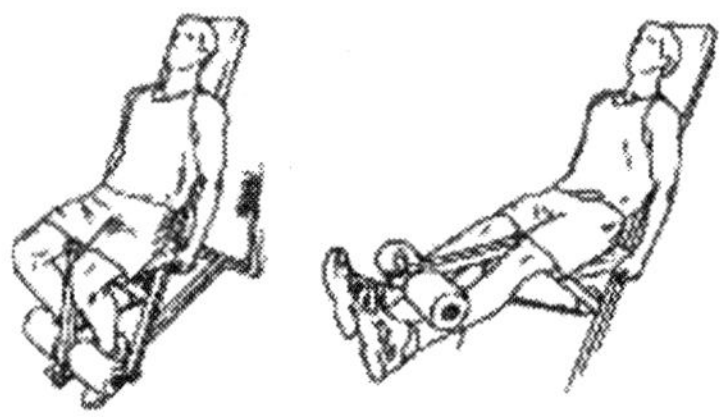
5. HIP ADDUCTION 

6. HIP ABDUCTION

LOWER-BODY CIRCUIT #3

Using Free Weights (Dumb bells, etc.)

If equipment or a weight you need isn't available or it feels uncomfortable doing a particular exercise, you can substitute the same number exercise from any of the other circuits.

1. DUMBBELL SQUATS

Standing erect, with your feet shoulder-width apart, your toes pointing slightly outward, and holding dumbbells at your sides, bend your legs to squat (no lower than thighs parallel with the floor) then return to full standing position.

2. HAMSTRING/BACK EXTENSIONS

With your feet secured, hang your upper body down over the end of a bench with your hands holding a light dumbbell behind your head. Raise the upper body until parallel with the floor.

3. CALF RAISES

With your forefeet supported on a low board and dumbbells held at your sides, raise up on your toes then slowly lower heels to the floor.

4. LUNGE SQUATS

Holding dumbbells at your sides, step forward with one foot, knee lowering toward the floor, and lifting your back heel off the floor. Alternate legs.

5. HIP ADDUCTION

Standing side on to a wall or bench for balance and using an ankle weight or tubing, draw your outside leg inward and across in front of the other.

6. HIP ABDUCTION

Standing side on to a wall or bench for balance and using an ankle weight or tubing, draw your outside leg up and away.

1. DUMBELL SQUATS

2. HAMSTRING/BACK EXTENSIONS

3. CALF RAISES

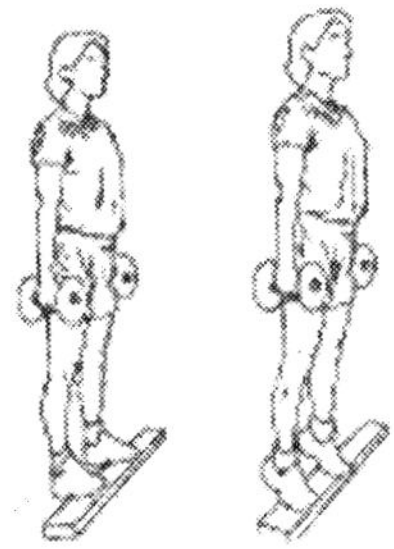

4. LUNGE SQUATS

5. HIP ADDUCTION

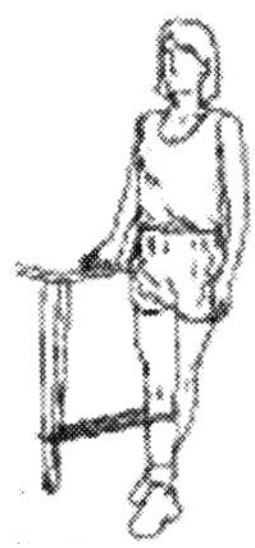

6. HIP ABDUCTION

LOWER-BODY CIRCUIT #4

Body-Weight Exercises

If equipment or a weight you need isn't available or it feels uncomfortable doing a particular exercise, you can substitute the same number exercise from any of the other circuits.

1. SQUATS

With your hands on your hips, squat (no lower than thighs parallel with the floor) then return to full standing position.

2. FRONT-SIDE LUNGE

Step forward and to the side (45°) with one leg, bending the leg and shifting your weight over it. Repeat alternately to the other side.

3. CALF RAISES

With your forefeet supported on a low board, raise up on your toes then slowly lower heels to the floor.

4. ONE-LEGGED WALL SQUATS

With one leg extended in front, support body weight on the other leg and slide the back down the wall until the supporting leg has a 90° bend.

5. HIP ADDUCTION

Lying on your side, rest the foot of your top leg on a bench about 30 cm high then pull your bottom leg up to the top one. Switch sides and repeat.

6. HIP ABDUCTION

Lying on your side, raise both your legs 10-15 cm while keeping the legs together. Switch sides and repeat.

1. SQUATS

2. FRONT-SIDE LUNGE

3. CALF RAISES

4. ONE-LEGGED WALL SQUATS

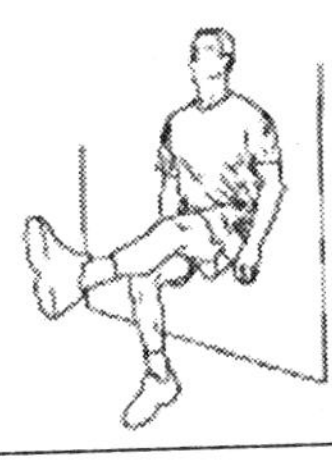

5. HIP ADDUCTION	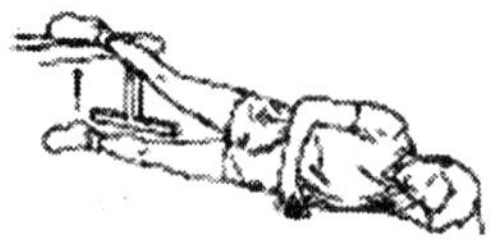
6. HIP ABDUCTION	

LOWER-BODY CIRCUIT #5

Partner-Resistance Exercises

If equipment or a weight you need isn't available or it feels uncomfortable doing a particular exercise, you can substitute the same number exercise from any of the other circuits. When working with a partner, give each other feedback on technique, proper resistance, etc.

1. RESISTED SQUAT

In squat position with a stick on your shoulders, partner resists from behind as you straighten legs returning to full upright position. Return to start position *without* resistance.

2. HAMSTRING CURLS

With partner resistance pull your heels up, bending your knees until your heels touch your buttocks.

3. CALF RAISES

With your forefeet supported on a low board and heels on the floor and a partner putting resistance on your shoulders from behind, raise up on your toes slowly to full extension. Return to starting position *without* resistance. (Partner can stand on a chair behind to push down from above if more resistance is required.)

4. DEAD LIFT

Standing with your legs bent, feet shoulder-width apart and toes pointing slightly outward, and your back straight (squatting), grasp a stick in front. Straighten your legs returning to full upright position with your partner providing resistance from below. Return to start position *without* resistance.

5. HIP ADDUCTION AND 6. HIP ABDUCTION

Soldier A pushes his/her feet *inward* while Soldier B resists, then Soldier B pushes his/her feet *outward* while Soldier A resists. Switch roles and repeat.

1. RESISTED SQUAT

2. HAMSTRING CURLS

3. CALF RAISES

4. DEAD LIFT

5. HIP ADDUCTION AND 6. HIP ABDUCTION

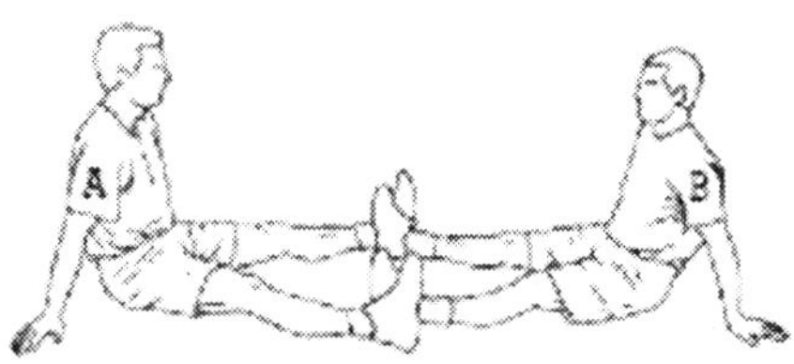

ABDOMINAL-CORE (ABCORE) CIRCUIT #1

Floor Exercises

- Keep your lower body stable with your feet flat on the floor. Use your abdominal muscles to lift and twist your upper body as shown in the sequence.

- When you get to position #6, continue to #1 and repeat the sequence.
- To begin, do the sequence (positions 1 through 6) 20 times for 1 set. Repeat 2 more times for a total of 3 sets of 20. Rest 2-3 minutes between sets.
- When you can do 3 x 20 comfortably, increase to 3 x 30, then again to 3x 40.
- When you can do 3 x 40 comfortably, move on to Circuit #2.

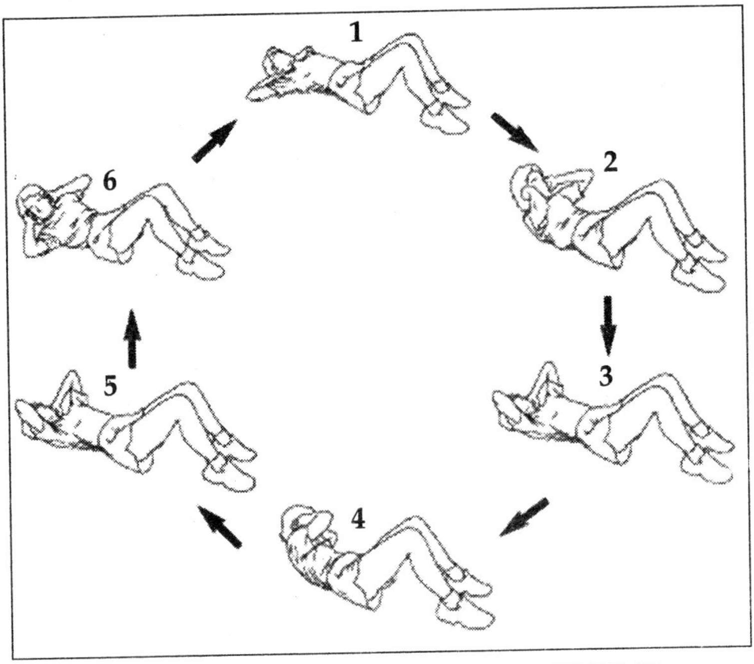

ABDOMINAL-CORE (ABCORE) CIRCUIT #2

Supporting on a Dip Bar

- Support your upper body on a dip bar to keep it stable. Use your abdominal muscles to move your lower body as shown in the sequence.

- When you get to position #6, continue to #1 and repeat the sequence.
- To begin, do the sequence (positions 1 through 6) 20 times for 1 set. Repeat 2 more times for a total of 3 sets of 20. Rest 2-3 minutes between sets.
- When you can do 3 x 20 comfortably, increase to 3 x 30, then again to 3 x 40.
- When you can do 3 x 40 comfortably, move on to Circuit #3.

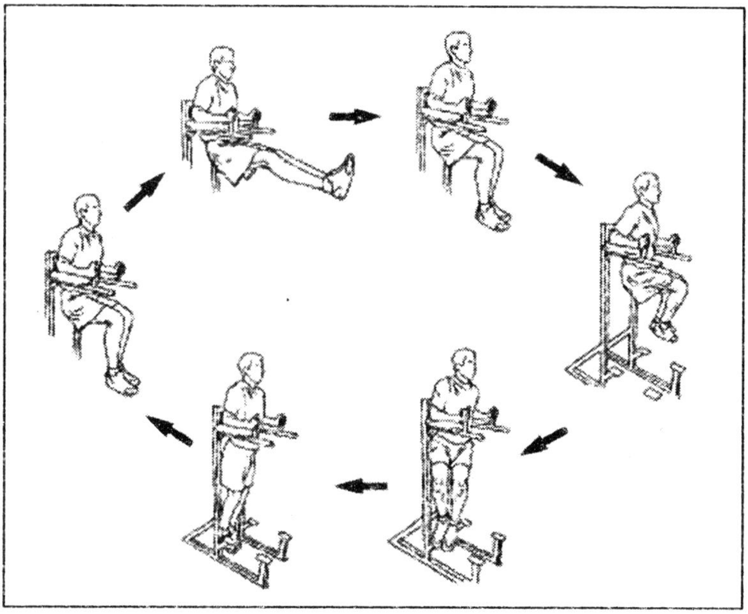

ABDOMINAL-CORE (ABCORE) CIRCUIT #3

Hanging from a Chin-up Bar

- Hang from a chin-up bar and keep your upper body in a stable position. Use your abdominal muscles to move your lower body as shown in the sequence.

- When you get to position #5, continue to #1 and repeat the sequence.
- To begin, do the sequence (positions 1 through 6) 20 times for 1 set. Repeat 2 more times for a total of 3 sets of 20. Rest 2-3 minutes between sets.
- When you can do 3 x 20 comfortably, increase to 3 x 30, then again to 3 x 40.

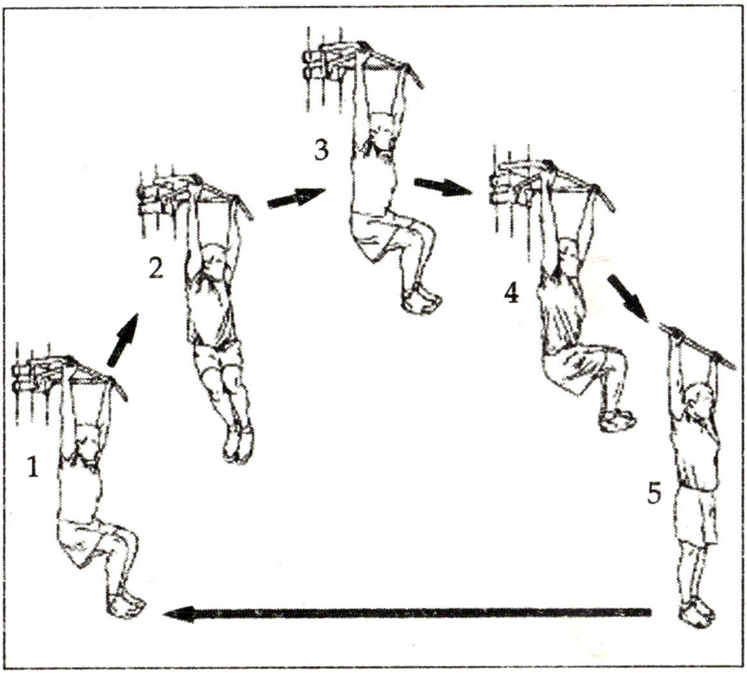

ABDOMINAL-CORE (ABCORE) CIRCUIT #4

Partner Plyometric Drills

- This is a demanding, dynamic routine, so do Circuit 1, 2, or 3 for the first two weeks of your programme before trying this circuit.

- Use a medicine ball for these exercises. Start with a light one and increase the weight gradually.
- Do 2 sets of 20 repetitions of each exercise during Weeks 3 to 6. Do 3 sets of 20 during Weeks 7 to 12.

1. SITTING CHEST PASS

Holding your upper body in a stable position, do push passes back and forth.

2. OVERHEAD PASS DOING SIT-UPS

Start with the ball overhead. Pass to your partner who lies down then does a sit-up returning the pass. Catch it, lie down, sit-up and return the pass yourself. Continue the sequence without pause.

3. STANDING SHUFFLE PASS

Pass the ball to your partner's opposite side. Twist as you pass and catch. Repeat on the other side.

4. CHEST PASS DOING SIT-UPS

Follow sequence as in #2 but doing chest passes instead of overhead ones.

5. 360° BALL PASS

Standing back-to-back with your partner, turn and hand the ball off then turn to the other side to receive it again. Repeat in the other direction.

1. SITTING CHEST PASS

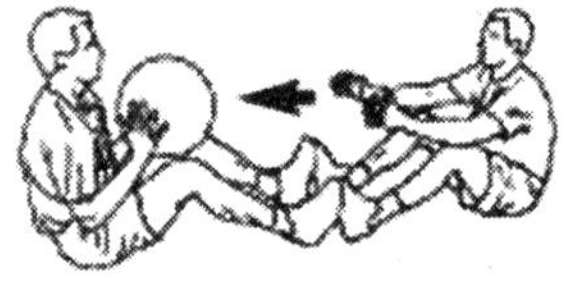

2. OVERHEAD PASS DOING SIT-UPS

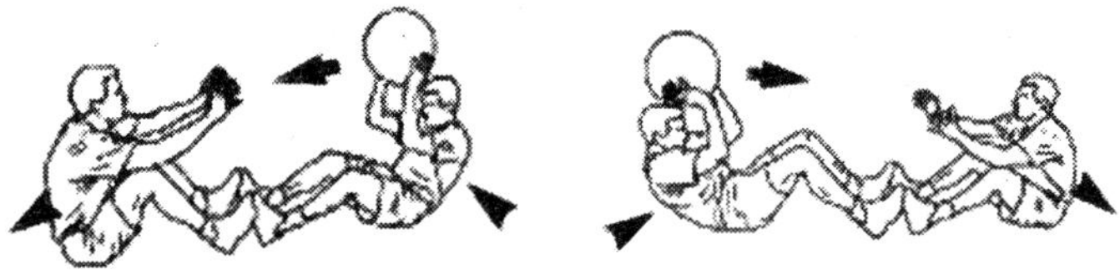

3. STANDING SHUFFLE PASS

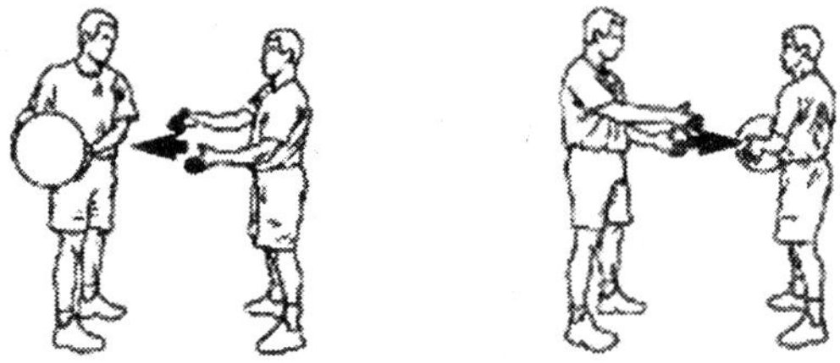

4. CHEST PASS DOING SIT-UPS

5. 360° BALL PASS

ALTERNATIVE EXERCISES

Here are some exercises using equipment like beams, ropes, logs, drums, and tyres. You could also use a jerry can, filling it with water to a level that gives the weight you need. You can do any of these exercises instead of ones in the circuits if you don't have stack weights or free weights available (remember the body-weight and partner-resistance exercises can always be done too). Each description notes which circuit/exercise it approximates. Do the reps and sets listed in your programme for that day.

For example, on each UB and LB strength-training day, you should do the six types of exercises described in each circuit. If you wish to substitute an alternative exercise, you can insert it in the regular circuit, replacing the specific exercise(s) noted in the alternative exercise description. The alternative exercises load a number of muscle groups in a single exercise rather than specific muscles like the regular circuits. This allows you to train more muscle groups with one activity but does not give as much load to any one group.

1. BEAMS

Bend arms to pull up, touching back of neck to the beam.

2. ROPES

Vertical rope climb without use of feet.

3. ROPES

Vertical rope climb using hands and feet.

ALTERNATIVE EXERCISES (CONT'D)

LOGS

Logs held chest high on palms of hands, extend arms forward.

LOGS

Knees bent, log held on shoulder, extend arms upward while straightening legs.

LOGS

Bend torso sideways away from log, reaching downwards with free hand. Bend torso sideways toward log with free arms reaching up and over.

DRUMS

Stoop and grasp drum in front, curl it in the arms and lift to full standing position.

DRUMS

Stoop and grasp drum on top edges, lift to full standing position with arms extended below.

TYRES/WHEELS

Stoop and grasp heavy wheel in front, straighten legs to return to full standing position.

LOGS

Stoop to grasp logs in front, lift to full standing position then press it overhead. Return to start position, bending the knees.

LOGS

Squat holding log at shoulder height.

LOGS

Hold log below with arms extended, then torso twist from side to side.

LOGS

Hold log horizontally below with arms extended, then lift it to upright position against one shoulder.

LOGS

Bent over and knees slightly bent, lift log to chest.

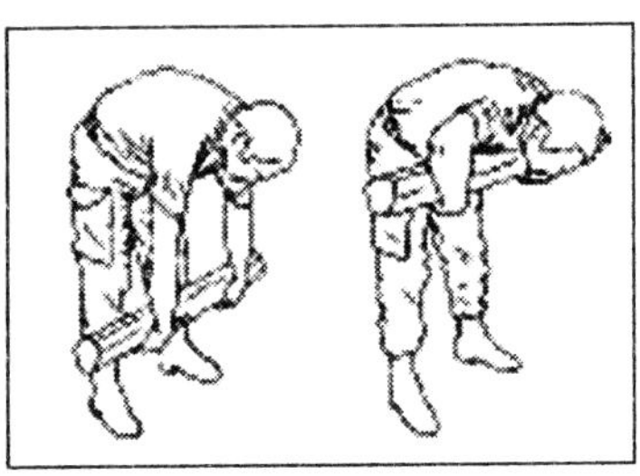

LOGS

Standing erect with log resting on shoulders, do squat to thighs parallel with the floor.

LOGS

Standing erect and log on shoulders behind the neck, press it overhead.

LOGS

Log resting on shoulders, bend torso side to side.

LOGS

Lift log upward, hand under hand, then lower it, hand over hand.

LOGS

Full standing position, stride jump, return to full standing position, then squat (until thighs are parallel with the floor). Repeat.

LOGS

Lying flat on your back, extend arms to press log above chest.

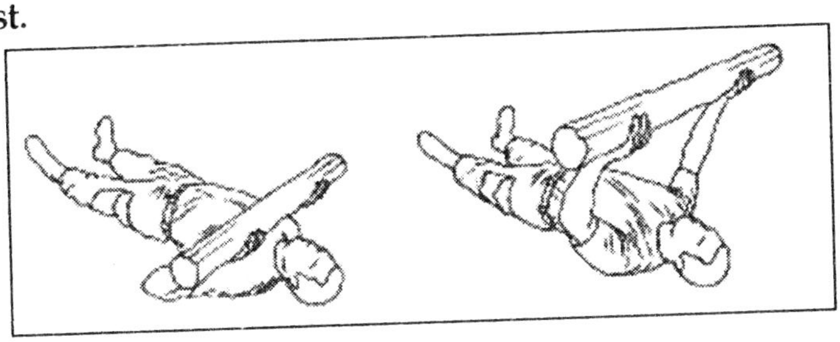

POWER AND SPEED TRAINING

There are three training routines included here:

- a plyometric circuit
- a sprint programme, and
- field exercises.

Do the routines on the required days as set out in the Training Prescription charts. Here are a few pointers:

- Review the Power and Speed *Set-Up* and *Doing It* information in the Training Principles chapter at any time if you need to refresh your memory.
- Do a *thorough* warm-up on the days you do these routines. They are challenging and dynamic, so you want to make sure your body is ready for them.
- Give a little extra attention to particular warm-up stretching exercises in the routine at the beginning of Chapter 5, as follows:
- on plyometric days: stretches #7, #8, and #10
- on sprint days: stretches #9 and #10
- on field-exercise days: stretches #2, #3, and #5
- Use the illustrations and descriptions provided to guide you in the right technique.

PLYOMETRIC CIRCUIT

Jumping and Bounding Routine

- Emphasize stretching exercises 7, 8, and 10 during your warm-up.
- Mark out a 20 m distance on a grass surface for Drills 1 to 4.

- Go through the circuit in sequence: Drill 1, walk back, Drill 2, etc., through to Drill 4, then for Drill 5 do the movement 6-10x.
- Use the illustrations as a guide for the proper movement.
- Repeat the circuit 2x during Week 4, then 3x after that.

1. Drill Jump from left foot to right foot straight down the line.
2. Drill Jump from right foot to left foot, crossing over the mid-line.
3. Drill Hop on same leg 4x, then other leg 4x.
4. Drill Double-leg jumps in straight line for 10 m, then double-leg jumps from side to side for 10 m.
5. Drill Stand on left leg and jump to the left, then stand on right leg and jump to the right.

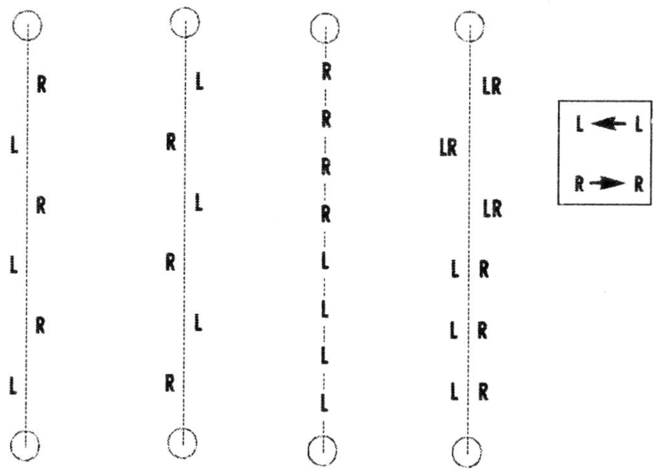

SPRINT PROGRAMME

Acceleration Running

- Emphasize **stretching exercises 9 and 10** during your warm-up.
- Mark out the required distances on a grass field, running track, or other firm surface.
- Do the combination of sets noted for each specific training session. These are shown in the **Training Prescription** charts.
- Follow each set with three minutes recovery (easy walking, stretching) before starting the next set.
- Accelerate from the start to the "all out" speed you can reach in the distance run.

1. SET Sprint 20 m then jog back *x 12,* then 3 minutes recovery.
2. SET Sprint 40 m then jog back *x 8,* then 3 minutes recovery.
3. SET Sprint 60 m then jog back *x 4,* then 3 minutes recovery.
4. SET Sprint 80 m then jog back *x 2,* then 3 minutes recovery.

FIELD EXERCISES

AFS Task Simulations

- Emphasize stretching exercises 2, 3 and 5 during your warm-up.
- Work with a partner. You will actually work together on the ammunition box lift-and-lower. On the other exercises, you can alternate work and rest intervals with your partner to pace yourself.
- Do a proper warm-up prior to these exercises. Lift and carry with care to protect your back.
- Do the combination of reps, sets, and loads noted in the Training Prescription table.
- Do the first set of each exercise (casualty evacuation, then ammunition box lift, then shovel drill), then repeat additional sets as noted.

1. CASUALTY EVACUATION

Measure out a course (in metres) as noted in the Training Prescription chart you are working on. Do fireman's carry with a partner of equal weight out and back the measured distance. Repeat for the number of times required for that session.

2. AMMUNITION BOX LIFT-AND-LOWER DRILL

Lift and lower a 20.9 kg box to a truck bed, shelf, table, or bench (1.3 m height). Working with your partner, you *lift* the box, then *your partner lowers* it back to the floor. Repeat this sequence for the required number of repetitions (e.g., 20), then change rolls (partner lifts, you lower). This constitutes *1 set*. Repeat for the number of sets required for that session. Rest two minutes between sets. Remember that there is a time limit for this task in the AFS so train to gradually prepare yourself for this. (1 box every 6 sec)

3. SHOVELLING DRILL

Using a standard (garden) shovel, move the gravel from one trench to the other. Go at a steady pace to conserve energy and to be efficient. Experiment to find your best pace, shovel load, and technique. Alternate with your partner, and repeat the number of times required for that session. For the AFS, the goal is to complete the task comfortably in less than six minutes.

6

Speciality Training Programmes

Chapter 3 details the full, 12-week Army Fitness Programme. It is the "gold seal" programme designed to bring your personal fitness level up to the Army Fitness Standard. There will be times and situations, however, where it will not be possible to work through a 12-week programme.

This chapter sets out four specialty programmes to address particular needs:

- an Eight-Week Garrison Programme
- a Six-Week Rapid-Deployment Programme
- a Three-Week Rapid-Deployment Programme
- a Four-Week Field-Training Programme.

EIGHT-WEEK GARRISON PROGRAMME

This programme sets out an *eight-week* garrison training routine. It is a modified version of the 12-week programme, designed for use when time does not permit the full programme or when it is necessary to coordinate the training with other activities or commitments.

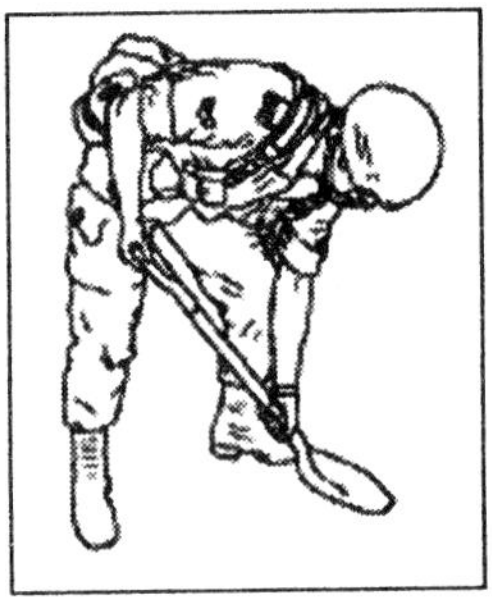

The weightload march and field exercises are important components of this programme, just as they are in the 12-week programme. The 8-week programme also includes continuous and interval aerobic sessions, strengthtraining circuits, and power/speed workouts.

THE SET-UP...

- Training takes place four days a week (Days 1, 2, 4, and 5) as set out in the *Training Schedule*.
- Day 6 is an *Optional* training day, depending on your need for additional fitness work balanced with your other tasks and responsibilities to the unit.

DOING IT...

Read the *Guidelines* to the right of the *Training Schedule* from beginning to end *before* your first session in Week 1.

- If you need to refresh your memory about any of the activities, read the appropriate chapters or sections earlier in the manual.
- Do a proper warm-up at the beginning of each training session and a cool-down at the end.

EIGHT-WEEK GARRISON TRAINING SCHEDULE.

For Weeks 1 to 4

	DAY 1 MONDAY	DAY 2 TUESDAY	DAY 3 WEDNESDAY	DAY 4 THURSDAY	DAY 5 FRIDAY	DAY 6 SATURDAY	DAY 7 SUNDAY
WEEK 1	Aerobic Fitness Check: 2400 m run Strength Check: push-ups	Strength Check: bench press, squats, sit-ups	ACTIVE REST or SPORTS DAY	Power Check: standing long-jump, 2-jump, 40 m sprint	Aerobic Check: 5 km run	REST	REST
WEEK 2	AEROBIC INTERVALS 1 min. work/ 1 min. easy x 12 STRENGTH AbCore: Choose one circuit	STRENGTH One UB Circuit, #3,4, 5 or UB AltEx Sets: 2 Reps: F-1 One LB Circuit: #2,4,5 or LB AltEx Sets: 1 Reps: F-1 POWER Sprint Programme Sets 1 and 2	ACTIVE REST or SPORTS DAY	STRENGTH One UB Circuit, #3,4, 5 or UB AltEx Sets: 2 Reps: F-1 One LB Circuit: #2,4,5 or LB AltEx Sets: 1 Reps: F-1 POWER Sprint Programme Sets 1 and 2	CONTINUOUS AEROBIC 34 min. "JT" STRENGTH AbCore: Choose one circuit	CONTINUOUS AEROBIC 34 min. "JT" STRENGTH AbCore: Choose one circuit — OR — STRENGTH One UB Circuit, #3,4, 5 or UB AltEx Sets: 2 Reps: F-1 POWER Sprint Programme Set 1 and Set 2	REST

	DAY 1 MONDAY	DAY 2 TUESDAY	DAY 3 WEDNESDAY	DAY 4 THURSDAY	DAY 5 FRIDAY	DAY 6 SATURDAY	DAY 7 SUNDAY
WEEK 3	AEROBIC INTERVALS 1 min. work / 1 min. easy x 15 STRENGTH AbCore: Choose one circuit	STRENGTH One UB Circuit, #3,4, 5 or UB AltEx Sets: 2 Reps: F-1 One LB Circuit: #2,4,5 or LB AltEx Sets: 1 Reps: F-1 POWER Sprint Programme Sets 1 and 2	ACTIVE REST or SPORTS DAY	STRENGTH One UB Circuit, #3,4, 5 or UB AltEx Sets: 2 Reps: F-1 POWER Sprint Programme Sets 1, 2 and 3	CONTINUOUS AEROBIC 38 min. "JT" STRENGTH AbCore: Choose one circuit	CONTINUOUS AEROBIC 38 min. "JT" STRENGTH AbCore: Choose one circuit — OR — STRENGTH One UB Circuit, #3,4, 5 or UB AltEx Sets: 2 Reps: F-1 One LB Circuit: #2,4,5 or LB AltEx Sets: 2 Reps: F-1	REST
WEEK 4	AEROBIC INTERVALS 1 min. work/ 1 min. easy x 17 STRENGTH AbCore: Choose one circuit	STRENGTH One UB Circuit, #3,4, 5 or UB AltEx Sets: 2 Reps: F-1 One LB Circuit: #2,4,5 or LB AltEx Sets: 1 Reps: F-1 POWER Plyometric Circuit	ACTIVE REST or SPORTS DAY	STRENGTH One UB Circuit, #3,4, 5 or UB AltEx Sets: 2 Reps: F-1 One LB Circuit: #2,4,5 or LB AltEx Sets: 1 Reps. F-1	CONTINUOUS AEROBIC 42 min. "JT" STRENGTH AbCore: Choose one circuit	CONTINUOUS AEROBIC 42 min. "JT" STRENGTH AbCore: Choose one circuit — OR — STRENGTH One UB Circuit, #3,4, 5 or UB AltEx Sets: 2 Reps: F-1 POWER Plyometric Circuit	REST

- For the Day 2 field exercises in Weeks 6 and 7, do the *first* set of each exercise (casualty evacuation, then ammunition box lift, then shovel drill), then repeat additional sets as noted.
- If you train on *Optional* Day 6, the specific programmes for you to follow are noted.

UB AltEx = Upper Body Alternative Exercises described on Page 108

LBAltEx = Lower Body Alternative Exercises described on Page 108

The numbers next to the Alternative Exercises refer to the number of the corresponding exercise in the Upper Body Circuit and Lower Body

Circuit. Any exercise may be substituted with an Alternative Exercise with the same number if equipment is not available.

GUIDELINES

FITNESS CHECKS

Nine items are completed in Weeks 1 and 8. Instructions for them appear in Chapter 4.

AEROBIC INTERVALS (DAY 1)

Level 1 – 200 m Level 2 – 225 m Level 3 – 250 m Level 4 – 275 m

CONTINUOUS AEROBIC (DAY 5)

Your approximate *"just talk"* or "JT" pace (in m/min) for your distance runs will depend on your level achieved in the 5 km run/Aerobic Check in Week 1 as follows:

Level 1–180 m/min Level 2–200 m/min Level 3–220 m/min Level 4–240 m/min

WEIGHTLOAD MARCH (DAY 5)

In Weeks 5, 6, and 7, these are done in full fighting order, including combat clothes, helmet, weapon, and rucksac. The distance and time (as well as the specific pace) for each march is noted.

STRENGTH TRAINING

The Abdominal-Core (AbCore) exercises are done in Weeks 1 – 4 on Day 1, Day 5, and Day 6 (Optional). You can choose from any of the four circuits.

The Upper-Body (UB) exercise circuit is done on Day 2, Day 4 and Day 6 (Optional).

The Lower-Body (LB) exercise circuit is done on Day 2 and Day 4.

Set the load that allows you to do the sets and reps noted. **Rather than** going to failure on each set, stop when you could still do one more rep (this is called "failure minus 1" or "F-1").

SPEED AND POWER TRAINING

The Plyometric circuit is done some weeks on Day 2 and Day 6 (Optional). The Sprint programme is done most weeks, generally on Day 2, Day 4, and/or Day 6. The Field exercises are added on Day 2 in Weeks 6 and 7.

DAY 6—OPTIONAL

First priority is Continuous Aerobic and Strength (AbCore) routines. Second priority is the Strength and Power routines.

EIGHT-WEEK GARRISON TRAINING SCHEDULE

For Weeks 5 to 8

	DAY 1 MONDAY	DAY 2 TUESDAY	DAY 3 WEDNESDAY	DAY 4 THURSDAY	DAY 5 FRIDAY	DAY 6 SATURDAY	DAY 7 SUNDAY
WEEK 1	AEROBIC INTERVALS 2 min. work/ 2 min. easy x 6 STRENGTH AbCore: Choose one circuit	STRENGTH One UB Circuit, #3,4, 5 or UB AltEx Sets: 2 Reps: F-1 One LB Circuit: #2,4,5 or LB AltEx Sets: 1 Reps: F-1 POWER Sprint Programme Sets 2 and 3	ACTIVE REST or SPORTS DAY	STRENGTH One UB Circuit, #3,4, 5 or UB AltEx Sets: 2 Reps: F-1 One LB Circuit: #2,4,5 or LB AltEx Sets: 1 Reps: F-1 POWER Sprint Programme Set 4	WEIGHTLOAD MARCH 5 km with 24.5 kg pack Time: 1 hr Pace = 5 km/hr	CONTINUOUS AEROBIC 40 min. "JT" STRENGTH AbCore: Choose one circuit — OR — STRENGTH One UB Circuit, #3,4, 5 or UB AltEx Sets: 2 Reps: F-1 POWER Plyometric Circuit	REST
WEEK 2	AEROBIC INTERVALS 2 min. work/ 2 min. easy x 7 STRENGTH AbCore: Choose one circuit	FIELD EXERCISES 5 sets each of: casualty evacuation 30 m out and back ammunition box lift/ lower x 20 reps shovel drill (30 full)	ACTIVE REST or SPORTS DAY	STRENGTH One UB Circuit, #3,4, 5 or UB AltEx Sets: 2 Reps: F-1 One LB Circuit: #2,4,5 or LB AltEx Sets: 1 Reps: F-1 POWER Sprint Programme Sets 3 and 4	WEIGHTLOAD MARCH 8 km with 15 kg pack (Time = 1 hr 30 min) Pace: 5.33km/hr	CONTINUOUS AEROBIC 40 min. "JT" STRENGTH AbCore: Choose one circuit — OR — STRENGTH One UB Circuit, #3,4, 5 or UB AltEx Sets: 2 Reps: F-1 POWER Sprint Programme Sets 3 and 4	

	DAY 1 MONDAY	DAY 2 TUESDAY	DAY 3 WEDNESDAY	DAY 4 THURSDAY	DAY 5 FRIDAY	DAY 6 SATURDAY	DAY 7 SUNDAY
WEEK 3	AEROBIC INTERVALS 2 min. work/ 2 min. easy x 8 STRENGTH AbCore: Choose one circuit	FIELD EXERCISES 6 sets each of: casualty evacuation 30 m out and back ammunition box lift/ lower x 20 reps shovel drill (30 full)	ACTIVE REST or SPORTS DAY	STRENGTH One UB Circuit, #3,4, 5 or UB AltEx Sets: 1 Reps: F-1 One LB Circuit: #2,4,5 or LB AltEx Sets: 1 Reps: F-1 AbCore: One circuit POWER Sprint Programme Set 4	WEIGHTLOAD MARCH 8 km with 24.5 kg pack (Time = 1 hr 30 min) Pace: 5.33 km/hr	CONTINUOUS AEROBIC 40 min. "JT" STRENGTH AbCore: Choose one circuit — OR — STRENGTH One UB Circuit, #3,4, 5 or UB AltEx Sets: 2 Reps: F-1 POWER Plyometric Circuit	REST
WEEK 4	AEROBIC FITNESS CHECK: 2400 m run STRENGTH CHECK: push-ups	STRENGTH CHECK: bench press, squats, sit-up	ACTIVE REST or SPORTS DAY	POWER CHECKS: standing longjump, 2-jump, 40 m sprint	AEROBIC CHECK: 5 km run	REST	REST

UB AltEx = Upper Body Alternative Exercises

LB AltEx = Lower Body Alternative Exercises

The numbers next to the Alternative Exercises refer to the number of the corresponding exercise in the Upper Body Circuit and Lower Body Circuit. Any exercise may be substituted with an Alternative Exercise with the same number if equipment is not available.

SIX-WEEK RAPID-DEPLOYMENT PROGRAMME

This section describes a six-week rapid-deployment programme to ensure that you are, at least, at the deployment Army Fitness Standard (AFS). The programme provides for the transition from garrison-style training to functional field activities. It is modeled after Weeks 7-12 of the Army Fitness Programme and is meant to fine tune an already satisfactory level of fitness.

The weightload march and field exercises are important components of this programme. It also includes interval aerobic sessions, strength-training circuits, and power/speed workouts.

THE SET-UP ...

- Training takes place four days a week (Days 1, 2, 4, and 5) as set out in the Training Schedule on the next two pages.
- Day 6 is an Optional training day, depending on your need for additional fitness work balanced with your other tasks and responsibilities to the unit. You or your commander can determine this week by week.

DOING IT ...

- Read the Guidelines from beginning to end before your first session in Week 1.

- If you need to refresh your memory about any of the activities, read the appropriate chapters or sections earlier in the manual.
- Do a proper warm-up at the beginning of each training session and a cool-down at the end.
- For the Day 2 field exercises, do the *first* set of each exercise (casualty evacuation, then ammunition box lift, then shovel drill), then repeat additional sets as noted.
- If you train on *Optional* Day 6, repeat the Day 1, 2, 4, or 5 routine, whichever focuses on your areas of greatest need.

SIX-WEEK RAPID-DEPLOYMENT TRAINING SCHEDULE

	DAY 1 MONDAY	DAY 2 TUESDAY	DAY 3 WEDNESDAY	DAY 4 THURSDAY	DAY 5 FRIDAY	DAY 6 SATURDAY	DAY 7 SUNDAY
WEEK 1	WEIGHTLOAD MARCH 8 km with 10 kg pack (Time = 1 hr 30 min) Pace = 5.33 km/hr STRENGTH AbCore: Choose one circuit	FIELD EXERCISES 5 sets each of: casualty evacuation 10 m out & back ammunition box lift/ lower x 10 reps shovel drill (10 half-full, 10 full)	ACTIVE REST or SPORTS DAY	CONTINUOUS AEROBIC 38 min. "JT" STRENGTH AbCore: Choose one circuit — OR — AEROBIC INTERVALS 1 min. work/ 1 min. easy x 15	STRENGTH One UB Circuit, One LB Circuit #3, 4 or 5: 2 sets of 15 RM for #3 and #5, 2 sets to failure for #4 AbCore: Choose one circuit	REPEAT either Day 1, 2, 4 or 5 — OR — REST	REST
WEEK 2	WEIGHTLOAD MARCH 8 km with 24.5 kg pack (Time = 1 hr 36 min, Pace = 5.0 km/hr)	FIELD EXERCISES 4 sets each of: casualty evacuation 20 m out & back ammunition box lift/ lower x 20 reps shovel drill (20 half-full, 20 full)	ACTIVE REST or SPORTS DAY	WEIGHTLOAD MARCH 10 km with 24.5 kg pack (Time = 2 hours, Pace = 5.0 km/hr)	FIELD EXERCISES 1 sets each of: casualty evacuation 100 m out & back ammunition box lift/ lower x 50 reps shovel drill (50 half-full, 50 full)	REPEAT either Day 1, 2, 4 or 5 — OR — REST	REST

	DAY 1 MONDAY	DAY 2 TUESDAY	DAY 3 WEDNESDAY	DAY 4 THURSDAY	DAY 5 FRIDAY	DAY 6 SATURDAY	DAY 7 SUNDAY
WEEK 3	WEIGHTLOAD MARCH 8 km with 24.5 kg pack (Time = 1 hr 30 min, Pace = 5.33 km/hr)	FIELD EXERCISES 3 sets each of: casualty evacuation 30 m out & back ammunition box lift/ lower x 25 reps shovel drill (30 half-full, 30 full)	ACTIVE REST or SPORTS DAY	CONTINUOUS AEROBIC 40 min. "JT" — OR — AEROBIC INTERVALS 1 min. work/ 1 min. easy x 17	STRENGTH One UB Circuit, One LB Circuit: 2 sets of 12 RM POWER Sprint Programme Set 1 and Set 2	REPEAT either Day 1, 2, 4 or 5 — OR — REST	REST
WEEK 4	WEIGHTLOAD MARCH 8 km with 24.5 kg pack (Time = 1 hr 20 min, Pace = 6.0 km/hr)	FIELD EXERCISES 3 sets each of: casualty evacuation 40 m out & back ammunition box lift/ lower x 30 reps shovel drill (30 full)	ACTIVE REST or SPORTS DAY	CONTINUOUS AEROBIC 42 min. "JT" STRENGTH AbCore: *Choose 1 circuit* — OR — AEROBIC INTERVALS 2 min. work/ 2 min. easy x 6 STRENGTH AbCore: *Choose 1 circuit*	STRENGTH One UB Circuit #3, 4 or 5: 2 sets of 10 RM POWER Sprints: 6 x 20 m every 10 sec 4 x 40 m every 20 sec 2 x 60 m every 30 sec	REPEAT either Day 1, 2, 4 or 5 — OR — REST	REST

	DAY 1 MONDAY	DAY 2 TUESDAY	DAY 3 WEDNESDAY	DAY 4 THURSDAY	DAY 5 FRIDAY	DAY 6 SATURDAY	DAY 7 SUNDAY
WEEK 5	WEIGHTLOAD MARCH 6.5 km with 24.5 kg pack (Time = 1 hour, Pace = 6.5 km/hr)	FIELD EXERCISES 3 sets each of: casualty evacuation 50 m out & back ammunition box lift/ lower x 35 reps shovel drill (40 full)	ACTIVE REST or SPORTS DAY	CONTINUOUS AEROBIC 45 min. "JT" — OR — AEROBIC INTERVALS 2 min. work/ 2 min. easy x 7	STRENGTH One UB Circuit, One LB Circuit #3, 4 or 5: 2 sets of 15 RM AbCore: Choose one circuit	REPEAT either Day 1, 2 or 5 — OR — REST	REST
WEEK 6	WEIGHTLOAD MARCH 10 km with 24.5 kg pack (Time = 1 hr 40 min, Pace = 6.0 km/hr)	FIELD EXERCISES 3 sets each of: casualty evacuation 60 m out & back ammunition box lift/ lower x 40 reps shovel drill (50 full)	ACTIVE REST or SPORTS DAY	CONTINUOUS AEROBIC 45 min. "JT" — OR — AEROBIC INTERVALS 2 min. work/ 2 min. easy x 8 STRENGTH AbCore: *Choose 1 circuit*	STRENGTH UB Circuit #3, 4 or 5: 2 sets of 12 RM POWER – Sprints: 2 x 20 m every 10 sec 2 x 30 m every 15 sec 2 x 40 m every 20 sec 2x 50 m every 25 sec 2 x 60 m every 30 sec	REPEAT either Day 1, 2, 4 or 5 — OR — REST	REST

GUIDELINES

CONTINUOUS AEROBIC (DAY 4)

Your approximate *"just talk"* or "JT" pace for your distance runs should be 220 m/min.

AEROBIC INTERVALS (DAY 4)

Approximate *distance* you will cover for each one-minute *work* interval is 250 m; for each two-minute work interval it is 500 m. For the easy recovery segment, you can jog, walk or stretch.

STRENGTH TRAINING

The Abdominal-Core (AbCore) exercises are done on Day 4 or 5. Choose one of four circuits.

The Upper-Body (UB) exercise circuit is done on Day 5. Choose from circuits 3, 4 or 5.

The Lower-Body (LB) exercise circuit is done on Day 5. Choose from circuits 3, 4 or 5.

Set the load that allows you to do the sets and reps noted. Remember, when training do not go to failure on any set. Stop when you can still do one more rep before failure (this is called "Failure minus 1" or "F-1").

SPEED AND POWER TRAINING

The **Sprint Programme** is done on Day 5. Special sprint routines are done on Weeks 4 and 6. They are outlined right on the chart.

DAY 6—OPTIONAL

If there is the opportunity to do additional physical preparation, the *Optional* day allows you to repeat either Day 1, 2, 4 or 5 from that week.

THREE-WEEK RAPID-DEPLOYMENT PROGRAMME

This programme provides for a transition from garrison to functional field activities with attendant increases in work capacity. It is modelled after Weeks 10-12 of the **Army Fitness Programme** and is meant to fine tune an already high level of fitness.

The weightload march and field exercises are important components of this programme. It also includes continuous and interval aerobic sessions, strength-training circuits, and power/speed workouts.

THE SET-UP...

- Training takes place four days a week (Days 1, 2, 4, and 5) as set out in the Training Schedule on the next page.

- Day 6 is an *Optional* training day, depending on your need for additional fitness work balanced with your other tasks and responsibilities to the unit. You (or your commander) can determine this week by week.

DOING IT ...

- Read the Guidelines to the right of the **Training Schedule** from beginning to end *before* your first session in Week 1.
- If you need to refresh your memory about any of the activities, read the appropriate chapters or sections earlier in the manual.
- Do a proper warm-up at the beginning of each training session and a cool-down at the end.
- For the Day 2 field exercises, do the *first* set of each exercise (casualty evacuation, then ammunition box lift, then shovel drill), then repeat for the second and third sets.
- If you train on *Optional* Day 6, repeat the Day 1, 2, 4, or 5 routine, whichever focuses on your areas of greatest need.

THREE-WEEK RAPID-DEPLOYMENT TRAINING SCHEDULE

	DAY 1 MONDAY	DAY 2 TUESDAY	DAY 3 WEDNESDAY	DAY 4 THURSDAY	DAY 5 FRIDAY	DAY 6 SATURDAY	DAY 7 SUNDAY
WEEK 1	WEIGHTLOAD MARCH 8 km with 24.5 kg pack (Time = 1 hr 20 min, Pace = 6.0 km/hr)	FIELD EXERCISES 3 sets each of: casualty evacuation 30 m out & back ammunition box lift/ lower x 30 reps shovel drill (30 full)	ACTIVE REST or SPORTS DAY	CONTINUOUS AEROBIC 40 min. "JT" STRENGTH AbCore: Choose one circuit — OR — AEROBIC INTERVALS 2 min. work/ 2 min. easy x 6 STRENGTH AbCore: Choose one circuit	STRENGTH UB Circuit #3, 4 or 5: 2 sets of 15 RM POWER Sprints: 5 x 20 m every 10 sec 4 x 40 m every 20 sec 3 x 60 m every 30 sec	REPEAT either Day 1, 2, 4 or 5 — OR — REST	REST
WEEK 2	WEIGHTLOAD MARCH 6.5 km with 24.5 kg pack (Time = 1 hour, Pace = 6.5 km/hr)	FIELD EXERCISES 3 sets each of: casualty evacuation 40 m out & back ammunition box lift/ lower x 35 reps shovel drill (40 full)	ACTIVE REST or SPORTS DAY	CONTINUOUS AEROBIC 45 min. "JT" — OR — AEROBIC INTERVALS 2 min. work/ 2 min. easy x 7	STRENGTH One UB Circuit, One LB Circuit #3, 4 or 5: 3 sets of 12 RM AbCore: Choose one circuit	REPEAT either Day 1, 2, 4 or 5 — OR — REST	REST

	DAY 1 MONDAY	DAY 2 TUESDAY	DAY 3 WEDNESDAY	DAY 4 THURSDAY	DAY 5 FRIDAY	DAY 6 SATURDAY	DAY 7 SUNDAY
WEEK 3	WEIGHTLOAD MARCH 10 km with 24.5 kg pack (Time = 1 hr 40 min, Pace = 6.0 km/hr)	FIELD EXERCISES 3 sets each of: asualty evacuation 50 m out & back ammunition box lift/ lower x 40 reps cshovel drill (50 full)	ACTIVE REST or SPORTS DAY	CONTINUOUS AEROBIC 40 min. "JT" — OR — AEROBIC INTERVALS 2 min. work/ 2 min. easy x 8 AND STRENGTH AbCore: Choose one circuit	STRENGTH UB Circuit #3, 4 or 5: 2 sets of 10 RM POWER Sprints: 3 x 20 m every 10 sec 3 x 30 m every 15 sec 3 x 40 m every 20 sec 2 x 50 m every 25 sec 2 x 60 m every 30 sec	REPEAT either Day 1, 2, 4 or 5 — OR — REST	REST

Study the Guidelines for each activity on the next page...

GUIDELINES

CONTINUOUS AEROBIC (DAY 4)

Your approximate *"just talk "* or "JT" pace for your distance runs should be 220 m/min.

AEROBIC INTERVALS (DAY 4)

Approximate *distance* you will cover for each two-minute work is 500 m. For the easy recovery segment, you can jog, walk or stretch.

STRENGTH TRAINING

The **Abdominal-Core (AbCore) exercises** are done on Day 4 or 5. Choose one of the four circuits.

The **Upper-Body (UB) exercise circuit** is done on Day 5. Choose from circuits 3, 4 or 5.

The **Lower-Body (LB) exercise circuit** is done on Day 5. Choose from circuits 3, 4 or 5.

Set the load that allows you to do the sets and reps noted. **Remember,** when training do not go to failure on any set. Stop when you can still **do one more rep before failure** (this is called "Failure minus 1" or "F-1").

SPEED AND POWER TRAINING

Special sprint routines are done on Day 5, Weeks 1 and 3. They are outlined on the chart.

DAY 6—OPTIONAL

If there is the opportunity to do additional physical preparation, the *Optional* day allows you to repeat either Day 1, 2, 4 or 5 from that week.

FOUR-WEEK FIELD-TRAINING PROGRAMME

This programme sets out a *four-week* routine to maintain your level of fitness when you are in the field. You will be familiar with all of the activities as they are drawn from the training programme outlined in detail earlier in the manual.

The weightload march and field exercises are important components of this programme. Strength-training circuits rely on the dumbbell, body-weight, and partner-resistance exercises. Activities that require stack weights or barbells are *not* included.

THE SET-UP...

- Training takes place four days a week (Days 1, 2, 4 and 5) as set out in the Field Training Schedule on the next page.
- Day 6 is an *Optional* training day, depending on your need for additional fitness work balanced with your

other tasks and responsibilities to the unit. You (or your commander) can determine this week by week.

DOING IT ...

- Read the Guidelines to the left of the Field Training Schedule from beginning to end before your first session in Week 1.
- If you need to refresh your memory about any of the activities, read the appropriate chapters or sections earlier in the manual.
- Do a proper warm-up at the beginning of each training session and a cool-down at the end.
- For the Day 2 field exercises, do the first set of each exercise (casualty evacuation, then ammunition box lift, then shovel drill), then repeat for the second and third sets.
- If you train on Optional Day 6, repeat the Day 1, 2, 4, or 5 routine, whichever focuses on your areas of greatest need.

FOUR-WEEK FIELD-TRAINING SCHEDULE

	DAY 1 MONDAY	DAY 2 TUESDAY	DAY 3 WEDNESDAY	DAY 4 THURSDAY	DAY 5 FRIDAY	DAY 6 SATURDAY	DAY 7 SUNDAY
WEEK 1	WEIGHTLOAD MARCH 8 km with 24.5 kg pack (Time = 1 hr 30 min, Pace = 5.33 km/hr)	FIELD EXERCISES 3 sets each of: casualty evacuation 20 m out and back ammunition box lift/lower x 25 reps shovel drill (20 full)	ACTIVE REST or SPORTS DAY	CONTINUOUS AEROBIC 38 min. "JT" STRENGTH AbCore: Choose one circuit — OR — AEROBIC INTERVALS 1 min. work/ 1 min. easy x 16	STRENGTH One UB Circuit, One LB Circuit #3, 4 or 5: 2 sets of 15 RM POWER Sprint Programme Set 1 and Set 2	REPEAT either Day 1, 2, 4 or 5 — OR — REST	REST
WEEK 2	WEIGHTLOAD MARCH 8 km with 24.5 kg pack (Time = 1 hr 20 min, Pace = 6.0 km/hr)	FIELD EXERCISES 3 sets each of: casualty evacuation 30 m out and back ammunition box lift/lower x 30 reps shovel drill (30 full)	ACTIVE REST or SPORTS DAY	CONTINUOUS AEROBIC 40 min. "JT" STRENGTH AbCore: Choose one circuit — OR — AEROBIC INTERVALS 2 min. work/ 2 min. easy x 6 STRENGTH AbCore: Choose one circuit	STRENGTH UB Circuit #3, 4 or 5: 2 sets of 12RM POWER Sprints: 6 x 20 m every 10 sec 4 x 40 m every 20 sec 2 x 60 m every 30 sec	REPEAT either Day 1, 2, 4 or 5 — OR — REST	REST

	DAY 1 MONDAY	DAY 2 TUESDAY	DAY 3 WEDNESDAY	DAY 4 THURSDAY	DAY 5 FRIDAY	DAY 6 SATURDAY	DAY 7 SUNDAY
WEEK 3	WEIGHTLOAD MARCH 6.5 km with 24.5 kg pack (Time = 1 hour, Pace = 6.5 km/hr)	FIELD EXERCISES 3 sets each of: casualty evacuation 40 m out and back ammunition box lift/ lower x 35 reps cshovel drill (40 full)	ACTIVE REST or SPORTS DAY	CONTINUOUS AEROBIC 45 min. "JT" — OR — AEROBIC INTERVALS 2 min. work/ 2 min. easy x 7 STRENGTH AbCore: Choose one circuit	STRENGTH One UB Circuit, One LB Circuit #3, 4 or 5: 3 sets of 10 RM AbCore: Choose one circuit	REPEAT either Day 1, 2, 4 or 5 — OR — REST	REST
WEEK 4	WEIGHTLOAD MARCH 10 km with 24.5 kg pack (Time = 1 hr 40 min, Pace = 6.0 km/hr)	FIELD EXERCISES 3 sets each of: casualty evacuation 50 m out and back ammunition box lift/ lower x 40 reps shovel drill (50 full)	ACTIVE REST or SPORTS DAY	CONTINUOUS AEROBIC 45min. "JT" — OR — AEROBIC INTERVALS 2 min. work/ 2 min. easy x 8 STRENGTH AbCore: Choose one circuit	STRENGTH UB Circuit #3, 4 or 5: 2 sets of 12RM POWER Sprints: 2 x 20 m every 10 sec 2 x 30 m every 15 sec 2 x 40 m every 20 sec 2 x 50 m every 25 sec 2 x 60 m every 30 sec	REPEAT either Day 1, 2, 4 or 5 — OR — REST	REST

Study the Guidelines for each activity on the next page…

GUIDELINES

CONTINUOUS AEROBIC (DAY 4)

Your approximate *"just talk"* or "JT" pace for your distance runs should be 220 m/min.

AEROBIC INTERVALS (DAY 4)

Approximate *distance* you will cover for each one-minute *work* interval is 250 m; for each two-minute work it is 500 m. For the easy recovery segment, you can jog, walk or stretch.

STRENGTH TRAINING

The Abdominal-Core (AbCore) exercises are done on Day 4 or 5. Choose one of the four circuits.

The Upper-Body (UB) exercise circuit is done on Day 5. Choose from circuits 3, 4 or 5.

The Lower-Body (LB) exercise circuit is done on Day 5. Choose from circuits 3, 4 or 5.

Set the load that allows you to do the sets and reps noted. Remember, when training do not go to failure on any set. Stop when you can still do one more rep before failure (this is called "Failure minus 1" or "F-1").

SPEED AND POWER TRAINING

The **Sprint Programme** is done on Day 5. Special sprint routines are done in Weeks 2 and 4. They are outlined right on the chart.

DAY 6—OPTIONAL

If there is the opportunity to do additional physical preparation, the *Optional* day allows you to repeat either Day 1, 2, 4 or 5 from that week.

PERSONAL TRAINING RECORD

To ensure maximum protection of the rights of CF members and their dependents under the Pension Act, soldiers should maintain a daily record of their authorized physical fitness programme activities. The **Personal Training Record** forms on the next two pages make it easy for you to do this.

Follow these instructions to get the most out of this recording system:

- Do not write on the Personal Training Record form in the manual.
- Make 12 photocopies of the Personal Training Record form on the front and back of the next sheet. Use these pages to record your progress during the 12-Week Army Fitness Programme.
- Put the sheets together in a booklet with a good cover to protect them. Write your name, address and telephone number on the cover or across the top of the first page so if your record goes missing it can be easily returned.
- Follow the Completing Your Personal Training Record guidelines to keep your records accurate and up to date.
- Photocopy additional pages of the Personal Training Record when you begin a new programme (e.g., Eight-Week Garrison Training, Six-Week Rapid-Deployment), add these new pages to your booklet, and use them to record your workouts.

Index

Abdominal-Core(AbCore)
circuit#1, 92
circuit#2, 93
circuit#3, 94
circuit#4, 95
exercises,32
strength, 65
Advanced Fitness Training Assistant (AFTA), 25
Aerobic activity, 18
Aerobic capacity, 9, 14
Aerobic controls(Day 1), 44,48
Aerobic fitness, 10, 53
Aerobic intervals (Day 4), 124, 129, 134
Aerobic intervals, 28
Aerobics, 27
AFS assessment, 12
AFS difference, 13
AFS task simulations, 109
AFS, 20
Alcohol,16
Ammunition Box Lift, 12, 54, 109
Army Fitness Programme, 10, 12, 14, 24
Army Fitness Standard, 11
Army Fitness Training Principles, 27
Army Operations Course (AOC), 25

Back extensions, 67, 76
Ball pass, 96
Barbell squats, 82
Basic Fitness Training Assistant (BFTA), 25
Bench press, 55, 67, 70, 73, 79
Bent-over row, 70, 79
Bent-over Dumbbell row, 73
Bicep Curls, 68, 71, 73, 79

Body weight, 9
Body weight exercises, 75
Box Stepping, 35
Breakfast, eat nutritious, 16

Calf extensions, 81
Calf raises, 83, 85, 88, 90
Casualty evacuation, 11, 13, 109,
CF EXPRES Programme,13
CF Weight Wellness Programme, 16
Chin-up bar, 94
Chin-ups (hands over), 76
Chin-ups (hands under), 76
Common Army Phase (CAP), 25
Continuous Aerobic, 28
Continuous Aerobic (day 4), 124, 129, 134
Continuous Aerobic(day 5), 44, 48

Dead lift, 70, 73, 91
Dip bar, 93
Dips, 76
Drums,101
Dumbbell Squats, 85

Equipment Issue Scale (EIS), 11
Exercises, alternative, 98, 100
Exercises, body weight, 88
Exercises, partner-resistance, 90
EXPRES Programme, 31

Female Soldiers, Special Guidance for, 14
Field exercises, 32, 33, 48, 106, 108
Field-Training Programme, four week, 130
Fitness, 9
Fitness checks, 24, 44, 48, 52, 55
Fitness maintenance, 36
Floor exercises, 92
Food Guide, 16
Front-side lunge, 88
Fuel for fitness, 16
Full fighting gear,11

Garrison Programme, eight week, 111
Good foods,16

Hamstring curls, 81, 83, 90
Hamstring/back extensions, 85
Healthy weight, 11
Hip abduction, 81, 83, 86, 89, 91,
Injury management,19
Injury prevention and safety, 17

Land Force Command Physical Fitness Standard, 13
Lat pull-down, 67, 79
Leg press, 81
Logs, 100, 102, 104, 105
Lower-body (LB), 29
circuit# 1, 80

circuit# 2, 82
circuit # 3, 85
circuit # 4, 88
circuit # 5, 90
strength, 65
Lunge squats, 83, 86

Military press, 70
Muscular strength, 9

Optional, 45, 49, 52, 116
Optional Training Day, 34
Optional (Day 6), 125, 129, 134
Partner Plyometric Drills, 95
Partner-Resistance Exercises, 78
Personal Training Record, 21, 32, 134
Plain sugars, 16
Plyometric circuit, 32, 33, 106
Plyometrics,19
Power and speed training,106
Pregnant soldiers, 15
Primary Leadership Qualification (PLQ), 25
Push-ups, 56
Push-ups (fingers forward), 76
Push-ups (hands wide), 76

Quad extensions, 81

Rapid-Deployment Programme, six week, 119, 125
Resisted squat, 90
Rucsack, 11
Run, 5 kilometre, 55
Run, 2400 metre, 55

Seated press, 73
Shoulder press, 67, 79
Shovelling drill, 110
Sitting chest pass, 96
Sit-ups, chest pass doing, 96
Sit-ups,overhead pass doing, 97
Soldiers, 9
Speed and Power Training, 45, 49,52, 116, 124, 129, 134
Sprint, 40 metre, 57
Sprint programme, 32, 33, 106, 108
Squats, 56
Squats, one-legged wall, 88
Standing long jump, 56
Standing shuffle pass, 96
Strength Training, 44, 48, 52, 116, 124, 134
Stretching, cool-down, 63

Training Prescription Chart, 37, 61
Trench (Maximal) Dig, 12
Tricep Extensions, 67, 70, 73, 79
Tyres/wheels,102

UB/LB Circuits, 31, 32
Upper-body (UB), 29
circuit, 1, 67

circuit#2, 70
circuit#3, 72
circuit#4, 75
circuit#5, 78
strength, 65
Warm-up and stretching, 62
Warm-up, specific, 63
Weightload March (Day 5), 116
Weightload March, 11, 13, 27, 28, 52
Weights, using free, 82, 85
Weights(Barbell), using free, 70
Weights (Dumbbells), using free, 72
Weights, using stack, 67, 80

NOTES

NOTES

NOTES

NOTES